LUMINOUS THOUGHTS

A JOURNEY FROM THE HEAD TO THE HEART

JATANLAL RAMPURIA

<u>Dedicated to-</u>

My father's three elder brothers

LOONKARAN RAMPURIA

(1900-1980)

GHEWARCHAND RAMPURIA

(1902-1971)

TILOKCHAND RAMPURIA

(1906-1971)

And To my Parents

SHREECHAND RAMPURIA

(1909-2001)

&

HULASI DEVI RAMPURIA

(1912-1969)

.

To whom I owe a lot

For their affection & loving care

AND

Whose very remembrance inspires me

to refine my thoughts & life.

Contents

Acknowledgements   *vii*

At A Glance   *ix*

Preview- By Dr. H. C. Gupta   *xi*

Preview- By Dr. Rishikesh Rai   *xiii*

Preface   *xv*

PART - I : Magic In Miniatures

  1. Awakening   3

  2. Bubbles   10

  3. Candles   20

  4. Cross Currents   29

  5. Dawn   40

  6. Experience   49

  7. Faith   58

  8. Fragrance   65

  9. Galaxy   73

10. Honey Dips   81

11. Insight   90

12. Inspiration   98

13. Life   106

14. Merry Go Round   113

15. New Horizons   121

16. Online   130

17. Pearls   137

18. Persistence   145

19. Politics   151

20. Rainbow   161

21. Spring Time   169

22. Sweet & Sour   176

Contents

23. Thoughts   187

24. Wisdom   197

25. Extras   207

26. Yours Forever   214

PART - II : Prose Is Architecture

27. For Me Not To Forget Ever   221

28. Honour The Time   225

29. I Have Not Failed   230

30. Outward To Inward To Onward   233

31. The Chess Of Whims & Pleasures   237

PART - III : Poetry Is Interior Decoration

32. Human Family   243

33. In Spite Of War   245

34. God's Flight   247

35. A Spiritual Journey   249

36. Wander-Thirst   251

37. To Remember Me   252

38. Mother   254

39. Only A Dad   256

The Book's Vision In A Picture   259

Author Bio   261

ACKNOWLEDGEMENTS

My Immense Gratitude to-

- Jayash Surana, My Daughter's Son
- Vaibhav Surana, My Son's Nephew

  ... for all their help and assistance in bringing forth this publication.

At A Glance

<u>LUMINOUS THOUGHTS</u>

An assembly of mesmerising quotations, soul touching poems and inspiring essays, the gravity and intensity of which will add a fourth dimension to your thoughts and overdrive your imagination churning out solutions and answers to all that comes along the way.

Part-I

Magic in Miniatures

Part-II

Prose is Architecture

Part-III

Poetry is Interior Decoration

Conceptualized, compiled and arranged by

Jatanlal Rampuria, ADVOCATE

[<u>Note</u>- The compiler has made ample efforts to accurately quote/cite the poems, sayings, thoughts and the respective people attributed to them as available in public domain. But still if any ommission/error has remained, it is regretted. Reader may also kindly verify through public sources online/offline if needed.]

Preview- By Dr. H. C. Gupta

This book is a singular, if not a unique, collection of life building, human-making, character-reforming and soul-elevating thoughts – thoughts that have endurance without death. One who will read and see, Rampuria identifying himself with the mind and conscience of the persons whose thoughts are composed in this, say, Gita of today, shall cull gems of wisdom gathered by the author from the Shastras, philosophers, poets and sages and shall find himself on a highway towards making his life, career and name and fame.

A wish fulfilled at its best, the compilation is a rare tribute by a son to his mother and father and to his father's elder brothers. Learner- friendly and simple but essential to know matter has been presented in an imaginative new layout and style under various symbolic and catchy heads. The world is over-crowded with books on discourses, morality and on the art of living, but this attempt is somewhat different from the lot around both in its selection of material as well as in its presentation and truly deserves a place much higher than the common platform.

Since I have been associated with Shri Rampuria right from the conception, inception and perfection of this work, I can justifiably avow that no compiler, to the best of my knowledge, has taken so much pains in brushing up, revamping and filtering his messages so as to make it both comprehensive and tempting. Resultantly, the quotes, poems, couplets and essays included are remarkably witty and energizing, precise and accurate and short and sweet.

Those interested in making their life worth being followed will find a place for this work on their personal library- shelf and on their study table as a panacea to all maladies of this commercialized and digitalized era. I am fully convinced that Shri Rampuria's labour will bear sweet fruits. I may assure every mindful and alert reader that he will find the book worth his time and money spent on it.

Dr. H. C. Gupta
Retired Professor and
Ex-Dean of Faculty of Arts, J.U. Gwalior (MP)
M-13, Chetakpuri,
Jhansi Road, Lashkar, Gwalior(M.P)-474002

PREVIEW- BY DR. RISHIKESH RAI

This book 'SPARKS OF WISDOM' , split in 3 parts, is a combination of beautiful thoughts in the shape of quotations, poems, couplets and essays by Sri J. L. Rampuria a writer and thinker. The quotes are sayings of renowned persons from different walks of life. These are not only thought provoking but a deep moralizing effect is also embedded into them. These are purifiers of one's conscience and retain great wealth of wisdom. Shri Rampuria has meticulously categorized these thoughts under various captions like Candles , Fragrance , Galaxy , Spring Time etc. and painstakingly garnered golden thoughts on the topics from various textual sources. Human life is replete with many pleasures and pains and one has to endure these as per his destiny. Quotes are the guides and give us insight in situations of indecisiveness.

The soul touching poems at the beginning of each chapter, the 8 poems in part III of the book and couplets aptly chosen and placed at the end of each chapter in part I of this book are truly decorating the architecture created by the mesmerising quotes in part I and the equally inspiring 5 essays written by Sri Rampuria in part II of the book.

Mr. Rampuria has penned many books and represents a tradition of erudite scholarship. He had deftly and judiciously chosen the topics from the enormous repertoire of sayings which affect human life in myriad ways. An undertone of Non-violence and sense of frugality can be found in the essence of these quotations.

These thoughts are priceless jewels which can illuminate human life. These sparks of wisdom can ignite the passion for the ultimate knowledge and supreme being.

I extend my heartfelt congratulations to Shri Rampuria for such a splendid effort. I am assured that this great effort will surely attract the attention of not only scholars but of everyone who desires to unearth the aesthetic and sublime feelings. The contents of this book are keys to a happy and pragmatic way of living.

Best wishes to Shri Rampuria for this great endeavour.

Dr Rishikesh Rai

Preface

MESSAGE FROM THE TWO ROSES

I completed my school education at my native place Sujangarh in Rajasthan. Sri Sitaramji Dadhich was a teacher in my school. He was also my home tutor for 5 years till the year 1955 when I passed my matriculation and came to Kolkata for further studies. After that whenever I went to Sujangarh, I used to meet my said teacher both on the day of my arrival at and on the day of my departure from Sujangarh.

It was 1st November 1989. I went to Sri Sitaramji's home to seek his blessings on the eve of my departure for Kolkata. Hanging on the wall of the room there, a lovely picture of a black rose with shining dewdrops on its petals in the background and an ornamentally carved seven word quotation in the front caught my attention. It read, **"A SINGLE ROSE CAN BE MY GARDEN".**

I left Sujangarh that night but those seven words did not leave me. They went on haunting my mind all through the night. My journey ended in the morning and with it ended my search for the meaning those words so proudly contained and so eagerly wanted to share with me.

It was a different dawn that day which opened before me a new vista–wide and panoramic. I suddenly learned that big things also come in small packages. My thoughts continued – A single rose can be my garden- See universe in atom. A single rose can be my garden- Be content with whatever little you possess and enjoy it as a complete fortune. A single rose can be my garden- Rejoice the satisfaction which comes from doing small things well. A single rose can be my garden- Make a thing of beauty bring you eternal joy. A single rose can be my garden- Live a virtuous life and leave this world with a smiling face.

The rose that I plucked on that day filled me with a sweet lingering fragrance and, contrary to the laws of nature, it went on getting more and more fresh in my mind with the passing of time. But no, that single rose cannot be my garden, I felt. I wanted a lot more. Obviously, from that day onward I started planting more and more saplings in my garden in the shape of meaningful sayings of great philosophers, poets, writers, thinkers and doers.

Years passed and then I met a rose again. This time with a red rose. It happened in Poddar court, Kolkata. On a board put on a tripod at 3rd

floor, there was a line written artistically in the background of a beautiful full grown red rose. It read **"WHEREVER YOU SEE UGLINESS, CREATE SOME BEAUTY"**. A seven word wonder again! It had a mesmerizing effect on me and, as if pulled by some invisible force, I often stood in front of that beautiful sight for a minute or two and always felt that rose searching in me if I understood its message and if I have seen that rose faithfully doing what it preaches.

I am happy that I made myself look at the tripod, that nicely printed board, that smiling rose and that divine message- **"WHEREVER YOU SEE UGLINESS, CREATE SOME BEAUTY"** and keep those seven words close to my heart forever. The two roses made me feel like being back in school with the black rose as my class teacher and the red rose as my home tutor. They taught me "Don't let small things pass you by".

I am happy again that I understood and realized that ugliness is not only in a piece of paper or a tea-Bhand or cigarette butt thrown here and there. But ugliness also means and consists in unholy and envious thoughts, in derogatory and hurting words and in malicious and deceitful conduct.

This book, split in three parts- Magic in Miniatures, Prose is Architecture and Poetry is Interior Decoration- contains mesmerizing phrases, soul touching poems and thought provoking essays and is my attempt to convince those two roses that I have understood their messages as also their wish to spread the fragrance of those messages far and wide.

I believe that the words traverse time and space and go on to make their homes in unknown people's hearts and minds. I hope, therefore, that the wit and wisdom of the words in this book too will find a lovely home in the hearts and minds of its readers.

SHUBHASTE SANTU PANTHAN!

JATANLAL RAMPURIA
Advocate & Yours Truly

PART - I : Magic In Miniatures

৵

A museum of high value phrases reflecting the wit and wisdom of some of the renowned philosophers, poets, writers, thinkers and doers.

৵

༉

~~~~~~

<u>OPENING QUOTE</u>

"*I believe in God, but not as one thing, not as an old man in the sky. I believe that what people call God is something in all of us. I believe that what Jesus and Muhammad and Buddha and all the rest said was right. It's just that the translations have gone wrong.*"

-John Lennon

~~~~~~

༉

I
Awakening

~~~~~~

"Yoga-yukto visuddhatma vijitatma jitendriyah
Sarva-bhutatm-bhutatma kurvann api na lipyate

[Translation: One who works in devotion, who is a pure soul,
And who controls his mind and senses
Is dear to everyone, and everyone is dear to him.
Though always working, such a man is never entangled.]"

-Bhagwad Gita verse 7

~~~~~~

- There is no revenge so complete as forgiveness.

-Josh Billings.

- An average person uses over 400 trees worth of paper in a lifetime. Let us pledge to save paper and make this a green world.

-NSDL

- The greatest use of a life is to spend it on something that will outlast it.

-William James

- Humility is to make a right estimate of oneself.

-Charles H. Spurgeon

- I have become my own version of an optimist. If I can't make it through one door, I'll go through another door or I'll make a door. Something terrific will come no matter how dark the present.

-Rabindranath Tagore

- My tool has always been humour because it's the most entertaining way to put any ideology across, and it's fun, and it's positive, and it's a healer.

-Goldie Hawn

- Forgive many things in others, nothing in yourself.

-Ausonius

- There is a wisdom of the head, and a wisdom of the heart.

-Charles Dickens

- Education is our passport to the future, for tomorrow belongs to the people who prepare for it today.

-Malcolm X

- The mind is not a vessel to be filled, but a fire to be kindled.

–Plutarch

- There is enough on earth for everybody's need, but not enough for everybody's greed

-Mahatma Gandhi

- Listening more than speaking reflects a whole state of mind. It is indicative of sincerity and humility. It is the essence of a fine character. So talk less, listen more.

-Maulana Wahiduddin Khan

- Beauty is only skin deep. Character and performance last.

-Byrd Baggett

- The virtuous damsel called decency will turn her back on men who indulge in the vile vice called drunkenness.

–St. Thiruvalluvar

- Be as critical of yourself as you are of others.

-Byrd Baggett

- Tradition is a guide and not a jailer.

-Somerset Bagget

- Patience strengthens the spirit, sweetens the temper, stifles anger, extinguishes envy, subdues pride, bridles the tongue.

-George Horne

- Mother Nature speaks in a language understood within the peaceful mind of the sincere observer. Leopards, cobras, monkeys, rivers, and trees; they all served as my teachers when I lived as a wanderer in the Himalayan foothills.

-Radhanath Swami

- We can't help everyone, but everyone can help someone.

-Ronald Reagan

- Few delights can equal the presence of one whom we trust utterly.

-George Mac Donald

- The risk of a wrong decision is preferable to the terror of indecision.

-Maimonides

- We must use time wisely and forever realize that the time is always ripe to do right.

-Nelson Mandela

- Be less curious about people and more curious about ideas.

-Marie Curie

- Put more trust in nobility of character than in an oath.

-Solon

- Nobody stands taller than those willing to stand corrected.

-William Safire

- Never let a serious crisis go to waste.

-Rahm Emanuel

- Saying a firm but polite 'NO' to something you do not want or which you cannot do may mean short-term pain, but may save a long term grief.

-M chandrasekaran

- There are two types of meeting difficulties; you alter the difficulties, or you alter yourself to meet them.

-Phyllis Bottome

- What a wonderful life I've had. I only wish I had realized it sooner.

-Collette

- Opening a school, instilling faith in moral values and in a virtuous life is preparing for shutting down a prison.

-Acharya Mahashraman

- Nature is part of us... The sun shines not on us, but in us. The rivers flow not past, but through us, thrilling, vibrating every fiber and cell of the substance of our bodies, making them glide and sing.

-John Muir

- We are the living graves of dead animals mercilessly slaughtered to satisfy our appetite. We never pause to wonder at our feasts.

-George Bernard Shaw

- The essence of lying is in deception and not in words. A lie may be told in silence, by equivocation, by the accent on syllabi, by the glance of the eyes attaching the particular significance to a sentence. All those kinds of lies are worse and harsher by many degrees than a lie plainly worded.

-Fran Lebowitz

- A man is never so in trial as in the moment of excessive fortune.

-M.K. Gandhi

- Having a sharp memory is a good quality of the brain, but the ability to forget the unwanted things is a far better quality of the heart.

–Anonymous

- When people are fanatically dedicated to political or religious faiths or any other kind of dogmas or goals, it's always because these dogmas or goals are in doubt.

-Robert M Pirsig

- Adapt or perish, now as ever, is nature's inexorable imperative.

-HG Wells

- Beware lest you lose the substance by grasping at the shadow.

-Aesop

- Every man is guilty of all the good he did not do.

-Voltaire

৪৩

~~~~~~

"OH! Why should the spirit of mortal be proud?
Like a fast-fleeting meteor, a fast-flying cloud,
A flash of the lightning, a break of the wave,
Man passes from life to his rest in the grave"

-William Knox

~~~~~~

৪৩

II
Bubbles

"**THE MAN IN THE GLASS**
When you get what you want in your struggle for self
And the world makes you king for a day,
Just go the mirror and look at yourself
And see what that man has to say.

It isn't your father or mother or wife
Whose judgment upon you must pass
The fellow whose verdict counts most in your life
Is the one staring back from the glass

He's the fellow to please, never mind all the rest,
For he's with you, clear to the end,
And you've passed your most difficult, dangerous test
If the man in the glass is your friend.

You may fool the whole world down the pathway of years
And get pats on the back as you pass,
But your final reward will be heartache and tears
If you have cheated the man in the glass."

-Peter Dale Wimbrow

OPENING QUOTE

ଊଓ

~~~~~~

"Your living is determined not so much by what life brings to you as by the attitude you bring to life; not so much by what happens to you as by the way your mind looks at what happens."

-Kahlil Gibran

ଊଓ
~~~~~~

BUBBLES

- My life is bubble, but how much solid cash it costs to keeps that bubble floating.

-Logan Pearsall smith

- I'm quite hopeful about life after death. It's life before death, I'm not terribly cheerful about.

-Alice Thomas

- We must learn to live together as brothers or perish together as fools.

-Martin Luther King Jr

- As a species, we've somehow survived large and small ice ages, genetic bottlenecks, plagues, world wars and all manners of natural disasters, but I sometimes wonder if we will survive our own ingenuity.

-Diane Ackerman

- People who take no pride in the noble achievements of remote ancestors will never achieve anything worthy to be remembered with pride by remote descendants.

-Lord Macaulay

- You may attract people by the quality you display, but retain people only by the quality you possess.

-Anonymous

- Every time you are tempted to react in the same old way, ask if you want to be a prisoner of the past or a pioneer of the future.

-Deepak Chopra

- Don't get burned twice by the same flame.

-Christian Kondo

- Positive attitude may not guarantee success, but negative attitude guarantees failure.

-Anonymous

- Most people don't grow up. Most people age. They find parking spaces, honor their credit cards, get married, have children, and call that maturity. What that is, is ageing?

-Maya Angelou

- Losing your way on a journey is unfortunate, but losing your reason for the journey is a fate crueler.

-Henry Wadsworth Longfellow

- Practical efficiency is common and lofty idealism is not uncommon; it is the combination that is necessary and that combination is rare.

-Theodore Roosevelt

- We are not creatures of circumstances; we are creators of circumstances.

-Benjamin Disraeli

- They may forget what you said, but they will never forget how you made them feel.

-Carl Fredrick Buechner

- A little neglect may breed mischief – for want of a nail, the shoe was lost; for want of a shoe, the horse was lost; and for want of a horse the rider was lost.

-Benjamin Franklin

- Failing to plan is planning to fail.

-Alan Lakein

- Strategy without tactics is the slowest route to victory. Tactics without strategy is the noise before defeat.

-Sun Tzu

- People who fight fire with fire usually end up with ashes.

-Abigail Van Buren

- The least deviation from the truth is multiplied later a thousand fold.

-Aristotle

- Intolerance, indolence, injustice, indifference, intemperance and ingratitude lead to deterioration, defeat and disaster.

-Richard Sneed

- The only thing worse than being blind is having sight but no vision.

-Helen Keller

- Truth is serious business. When criticizing others, remember that a little goes a long way.

-H. Jackson Brown Jr

- The word 'revolution' is a word for which you kill, for which you die, for which you send the laboring masses to their deaths; but which does not contain any content.

-Simone Weil

- Who gossips with you will gossip about you.

-Turkish Proverb

- People who cannot find time for recreation are obliged sooner or later to find time for illness.

-John Wanamaker

- Those who will not reason, are bigots; those who cannot, are fools, and those who dare not, are slaves.

-Lord Byron

- Those who resist change will become irrelevant in the 21st century.

-Narendra Damordas Modi

- Temptation comes as a passer-by. It knocks on the door of the heart and wishes to be admitted as a guest. If you let it in, it will stay as a master.

-Prophet Muhammad

- While we are postponing, life speeds by.

–Seneca

- Those who own much have much to fear.

-Rabindranath Tagore

- Nothing is so exhausting as indecision, and nothing is so futile.

-Bertrand Russell

- Whatever you want to do, do it now. There are only so many tomorrows.

-Michael London

- Delays have dangerous ends.

–Proverb

- You could do great things if you weren't so busy doing little things.

–Anonymous

- The true test of a man's character is what he does when no one is watching.

-John Wooden

- Speak when you are angry and you will make the best speech you will ever regret.

-Ambrose Bierce

- Doing nothing is being ready to do mischief.

-John Ruskin

- Beware of little expenses; a small leak will sink a great ship.

-Benjamin Franklin

- For that man is detested by me at the gates of hell, whose outward words conceal his inmost thoughts.

–Homer

- If you buy things you do not need, soon you will have to sell things you need.

-Warren Buffett

- There is no activity in our society in which time, wealth and energy are not cheerfully massacred.

-Anonymous

- Beware the fury of a patient man.

-John Dryden

- Anger is momentary madness, so control your passion or it will control you.

-Horace smith

- Society prepares the crime; the criminal commits it.

-Henry Thomas Buckle

- If a man takes no thought about what is distant, he will find sorrow near at hand.

–Confucius

- All the crimes on earth do not destroy so many of the human race, nor alienate so much property, as drunkenness.

-Lord Bacon

- A teacher, who is attempting to teach without inspiring the pupil with a desire to learn, is hammering a cold iron.

-Horace Mann

- Remember that when your mother says, you will regret, you probably will.

–Anonymous

- Doubt the man who swears to his devotion.

  -Madame Louise Colet

- The world is disgracefully managed and one hardly knows to whom to complain.

  -Ronald Firbank

- Forget fundamentals; bubble will decide when to burst.

  -M.C. Govardhana Rangan

- Be faithful to that which exists within yourself.

  -Andre Gide

- When there is no peril in the fight there is no glory in the triumph.

  -Pierre Rneille Co

- A good name, like goodwill, is got by many actions and lost by one.

  -Lord Jefery

- When the power of love overcomes the love of power the world will know peace.

  -Jimi Hendrix

- We are forced to participate in the games of life before we can possibly learn how to use the options in the rules governing them.

  -Johann Wolfgang Von Geothe

- If you pray for rain long enough, it eventually does fall. If you pray for floodwaters to abate, they eventually do. The same happens in the absence of prayers.

-Steve Allen

- All know the way; few actually walk it.

–Bodhidharma

- We have to learn to cherish this earth and cherish it as something that's fragile, that's only one, it's all we have. We have to use our scientific knowledge to correct the dangers that have come from science and technology.

-Margaret Mead

ॐ

"When life is woe

And hope is dumb,

The world says, 'go!'

The grave says, 'come!'"

-Arthur Guiterman

ॐ

III
Candles

["]*PSALM OF LIFE*

Tell me not, in mournful numbers,
Life is but an empty dream!
For the soul is dead that slumbers,
And things are not what they seem.

Life is real! Life is earnest!
And the grave is not its goal;
Dust thou art, to dust returnest,
Was not spoken of the soul.

Not enjoyment, and not sorrow,
Is our destined end or way;
But to act, that each tomorrow
Finds us further than today.

Art is long, and time is fleeting,
And our hearts, though stout and brave,
Still, like muffled drums, are beating
Funeral marches to the grave.

In the world's broad field of battle,
In the bivouac of life,
Be not like dumb, driven cattle!
Be a hero in the strife!

Trust no future, however pleasant!
Let the dead past bury its dead!
Act, act in the living present!
Heart within, and god o'erhead!

Lives of great men all remind us
We can make our lives sublime,
And, departing, leave behind us
Footprints on the sands of time;

Footprints, that perhaps another,
Sailing o'er life's solemn main,
A forlorn and shipwrecked brother,
Seeing, shall take heart again.

Let us then be up for doing,
With a heart for any fate;
Still achieving, still pursuing,
Learn to labour and to wait."

-Henry Wadsworth Longfellow

ඥ

OPENING QUOTE

෫෮

~~~~~~

"Years may wrinkle the skin, but to give up interest wrinkles the soul. You are as young as your faith, as old as your doubt; as young as your self-confidence, as old as your fear; as young as your hope, as old as your despair. In the central place of every heart there is a recording chamber. So long as it receives messages of beauty, hope, cheer and courage, so long are you young. When your heart is covered with the snows of pessimism and the ice of cynicism, then, and then only, are you grown old. And then, indeed you just fade away."

-Douglas Macarthur

~~~~~~

෫෮

CANDLES

- One should not injure, subjugate, enslave, torture, or kill any animal, living being, organism, or sentient being. This doctrine of nonviolence is immaculate, immutable, and eternal.

-Acarangasutra 4.25-26

- I am absolutely convinced that to return evil for evil leads in nowhere. To return good for good is no virtue. The true way is to return good for evil.

-M.K. Gandhi

- Non-violence leads to highest ethics which is the goal of all evolution. Until we stop harming all other living beings, we are still savages.

-Thomas Alva Edison

- Everyone must leave something behind when he dies, my grandfather said. A child or a book or a painting or a house or a wall built or a pair of shoes made, or a garden planted. Something your hand touched some way or your soul has somewhere to go when you die, and when people look at that tree or that flower you planted, you're there.

-Ray Bradbury

- Don't say you don't have enough time. You have the same number of hours per day as all the great thinkers and all the great doers in the world had.

–Anonymous

- Discovery consists of seeing what everybody has seen and thinking what nobody has thought.

-Albert Szent Gyorgyi

- Vision is the art of seeing what is invisible to others.

-Jonathan Swift

- Books are the quietest and most constant of friends. They are the most accessible and wisest of counsellors and the most patient of teachers.

-Charles William Eliot

- We can't direct the wind, but we can adjust the sails.

-Thomas S. Monson

- You can't stop the birds of sorrow from flying over your head, but you can prevent them from building nest in your heart.

-Chinese Proverb

- Worry is a misuse of imagination.

-Dan Zadra

- If we had no faults, we should not take so much pleasure in noticing them in others.

-Francois de La Rochefoucauld

- There is no finer investment for any community than putting milk in babies.

-Winston Churchill

- Always remember to be happy because you never know who's falling in love with your smile.

-Anonymous

- The supreme excellence is not to win a hundred victories in a hundred battles. The supreme excellence is to subdue the armies of your enemies without even having to fight them.

-Lao Tzu

- Dost thou love life, then do not squander time, for that's the stuff life is made of.

-Benjamin Franklin

- Use what talents you have. The woods would be silent if no birds sang there except those that sang best.

-Henry Van Dyke

- The worst sin towards our fellow creatures is not to hate them, but to be indifferent with them.

-George Bernard Shaw

- Never mistake knowledge for wisdom. One helps you make a living; the other helps you make a life.

-Sandra Carey

- When you lose, don't lose the lesson.

-Dalai lama

- If you want to do something and you feel in your bones that it's the right thing to do, do it. Intuition is often as important as the facts.

–Anonymous

- Ask yourself if what you are doing today will guide you to what you want to be tomorrow.

-Walt Disney

- Every student requires a strong and healthy physique and sound character and a brain full of useful information and healthy, dynamic ideas.

-Subhash Chandra Bose

- We must have life-building, man-making, character-reforming assimilation of ideas.

-Swami Vivekananda

- Life is like a game of playing cards. The cards you get is your luck; a chance. How you play them, is your choice.

-Jawaharlal Nehru

- Better do a kindness near home than go far to burn incense.

-Chinese Proverb

- Life is too short to be spent in fault-finding, holding grudges or keeping memories of wrongs done to us.

-Dada J.P. Vaswani

- Look backward with gratitude, upward with confidence and forward with hope.

–Proverb

- Everyday, show your family how much you love them with your words, with your touch and with your thoughtfulness.

-H. Jackson Brown Jr

- To bring up a child in the way he should go, travel that way yourself once in a while.

-Josh Billings

- Be an original. If that means being a little eccentric, so be it.

–Anonymous

- A wise physician said-" The best medicine for humans is "care and love'!" Someone asked- what if it doesn't work? He smiled and answered "Increase the Dose".

–Anonymous

- Don't raise your voice. Improve your arguments.

-Desmond Tutu

- Terminating overlong conversations, lengthy interviews and unnecessary interruptions without this being felt by the person involved is a skill to be perfected: Not allowing others to steal our time is important.

-Anonymous

- Never throw mud. You may miss your mark; but you must have dirty hands.

-Joseph Parker

- Don't work for recognition, but do work worthy of recognition.

-H. Jackson Brown Jr

- Let your word be your bond.

-Anonymous

- In fair weather prepare for foul

-Thomas Fuller

- It is not only what we do, but also what we do not do, for which we are accountable.

–Moliere

- Remember no one makes it alone. Have a grateful heart and be quick to acknowledge those who help you.

-Anonymous

~~~~~~

"TRUTH
Man with his burning soul
Has but an hour of breath
To build a ship of truth
In which his soul may sail
Sail on the sea of death
For death takes toll
Of beauty, courage, youth
OF ALL BUT TRUTH"

-John Masefield

~~~~~~

IV
Cross Currents

*"**HE OLD, OLD SONG***
When all the world is young, lad,
And all the trees are green;
And every goose a swan, lad,
And every lass a queen;
Then hey for boot and horse, lad,
And round the world away;
Young blood must have its course, lad,
And every dog his day.
When all the world is old, lad,
And all the trees are brown:
All the sport is stale, lad,
And all the wheels run down:
Creep home and take your place there.
The spent and maimed among:
God grant you find one face there
You loved when all was young."

-Charles Kingsley

OPENING QUOTE

ೞ

~~~~~~

"*The pink and red of the dawn are the same in the twilight of the evening, but they are different from the root and different in their message. One says, 'Wake up'; the other says, 'Sum up'. Like dawn and dusk, many happenings in life do not reveal themselves in their appearance. They need to be read from inside out to get to the message they contain.*"

-Shreechand Rampuria

~~~~~~

ೞ

CROSS CURRENTS

- Prejudice, a dirty word, and faith, a clean one, have something in common: they both begin where ends.

  -Harper Lee

- The worst kind of loneliness in the world is the isolation that comes from being misunderstood.

  -Dan Brown

- For the most of us, if we do not talk of ourselves, or at any rate of the individual circles of which we are the centres, we can talk of nothing. I cannot hold with those who wish to put down the insignificant chatter of the world.

  -Lionel Trilling

- Not all crime is vulgar, but all vulgarity is crime.

  -Oscar Wilde

- The smallest good deed is better than the grandest intention.

  –Proverb

- They who pray only when in trouble at least know where to turn for help.

  –Anonymous

- Insults are like bad coins. You cannot avoid getting them but you can always refuse to accept them.

  -Dada J.P. Vaswani

- Risk comes from not knowing what you are doing.

-Warren Buffet

- Men have sight, woman insight.

-Victor King

- Hypocrisy, the only evil that walks invisible.

-John Milton

- 'He means well' is useless unless he does well.

-Titus Maccius Plautus

- Law grinds the poor, and the rich men rule the law.

-Oliver Goldsmith

- The true measure of a man is how he treats someone who can do him absolutely no good.

-Ann Landers

- In the practice of tolerance, one's enemy is the best teacher.

-Dalai Lama

- If you would lift me up, you must be on higher ground.

-Ralph Waldo Emerson

- A closed mouth catches no flies.

-Proverb

- The foolish man seeks happiness in the distance, the wise grows it under his feet.

-Julius Robert Oppenheimer

- Every child comes with the message that god is not yet disappointed of man.

-Rabindranath Tagore

- The only fence against the world is a thorough knowledge of it.

-John Locke

- Whatever precautions you take so the photograph will look like this or like that, there comes a moment, when the photograph surprises you. It is the other's gaze that wins out and decides.

-Jacques Derrida

- If you want to walk fast, walk alone. But if want to walk far, walk together.

-Ratan Tata

- Remember, today is the tomorrow you worried about yesterday.

-Dale Carnegie

- It is not enough to have a good mind; the main thing is to use it well.

-Rene Descartes

- Every burned book or house enlightens the world; every suppressed or expunged word reverberates through the earth from side to side.

-Ralph Waldo Emerson

- He that dies pays all the debts.

-William Shakespeare

- Our desires always increase with our possessions. The knowledge that something remains yet unenjoyed impairs our enjoyment of the good before us.

-Samuel Johnson

- It is a great misfortune neither to have enough wit to talk well nor enough judgment to be silent.

-La Bruyere

- Enemy-occupied territory is what the world is.

-C.S Lewis

- In nature there are neither rewards nor punishments; there are consequences.

-Robert Green Ingersoll

- Only the wisest and stupidest of men never change.

–Confucius

- It is not that they can't see the solution. It is that they can't see the problem.

-Gilbert K Chesterton

- Everybody is ignorant, only on different subjects.

-Will Rogers

- It is easier to forgive an enemy than to forgive a friend.

-William Blake

- In life you are either a passenger or a pilot. What you want to be is your choice.

–Anonymous

- A communist is someone who has read KARL Marx; an anti-communist is someone who has understood him.

–Under Ground under Soviet Era Joke

- We play many roles in our lives: if they get mixed up it becomes dark, like when you mix all the colors. Play each role distinctively side by side, like the colors displayed side by side.

-Sri Sri Ravi Shankar

- Be patient with a book. Unlike TV shows and games, books do not grab attention from the first page.

-The Telegraph 11th June, 2017

- Education's purpose is to replace an empty mind with an open one.

-Malcolm Forbes

- It is not in the stars to hold our destiny but ourselves.

-William Shakespeare

- Those who do not remember the past are condemned to repeat it. We must welcome the future, remembering that soon it will be the past; and we must respect the past, remembering that it was once all that was humanly possible.

-George Santayana

- As man draws nearer to the stars, why should he not also draw nearer to his neighbor?

-Lyndon B Johnson

- Whatever needs to be maintained through force is doomed.

-Henry Miller

- Our lives are like islands in the sea. Or like trees in the forest. The maple and the pine may whisper to each other with their leaves...but the trees also co-mingle their roots in the darkness underground and the islands also hang together through the ocean's bottom.

-William Janes

- It has always seemed strange to me...the things we admire in men, kindness and generosity, openness, honesty, understanding and feeling, are the concomitants of failure in our system.

-John Steinbeck

- Everything we see hides another thing; we always want to see what is hidden by what we see.

-Anonymous

- The right to do something does not mean that doing it is right.

-William Safire

- Always remember everything is easy when you are crazy about it, and nothing is easy when you are lazy about it.

-Anonymous

- How do you convince the upcoming generations that education is the key to success, when we are surrounded by poor graduates and rich criminals?

-Anonymous

- Everything is valuable only in two situations, first before getting it, second after losing it. In between we don't realize the value of anything.

-Anonymous

- Experience is hard teacher because it gives the test first, the lesson afterwards.

-Vemon Law

- He who has a 'WHY' to live, can bear with almost any 'HOW'.

-Friendrich Nietzsche

- A friend is someone who is there for you when he would rather be anywhere else.

-Booker T Washington

- What upsets me is not that you lied to me, but from now on, I can no longer believe you.

-Anonymous

- Sometimes the bad things that happen in our lives put us directly on the path to the best things that will ever happen to us.

-Anonymous

- Just because you are right doesn't mean I am wrong, you just haven't seen life from my side.

-Anonymous

- An opportunity is like biscuit dipped in tea, a little delay and its gone.

-Anonymous

- A bend in the road is not the end of the road, unless you fail to make the turn.

-Anonymous

- Company of good people is like walking in a shop of perfume, whether you buy the perfume or not, you are bound to receive the fragrance.

-Anonymous

- Two things to remember in life take care of your thoughts when you are alone, and take care of your words when you are with people.

-Anonymous

- Mistakes can always be forgiven if only you have the courage to admit them.

-Bruce Lee

- I don't know if there are men on the moon, but if there are they must be using the earth as their lunatic asylum.

-George Bernard Shaw

- We contend that for a nation to try to tax itself into prosperity is like a man standing in a bucket and trying to lift himself up by the handle.

-Winston S Churchill

- Every time a youngster resorts to violence, it is his family which suffers the most.

-Mehbooba Mufti

- We don't see things as they are; we see them as we are.

–Anaisnin

- Words should be weighed and not counted.

-Yiddish Saying

- Beautiful people are not always good, but good people are always beautiful.

-Saint Mother Teresa

- It is better to be feared than loved, if you cannot be both.

-Niccolo Machiavelli

- No man has a good enough memory to be a successful liar.

-Abraham Lincoln

- Two things define you. Your patience when you have nothing and your attitude when you have everything.

-George Bernard Shaw

౮౦

~~~~~~

"GOOD AND BAD
There is so much good in the worst of us,
And so much bad in the best of us,
That it still behoves any of us
*To find fault with the rest of us.***"**

-Anonymous

~~~~~~

V
Dawn

"BE NOT DOWNCAST OR DEJECTED

Be not downcast and dejected, O my heart!
Not even if indiscriminate
And inscrutable seem
The mercies and mortifications of Fate.
Do not ever circumscribe
The free heavens of thy wing
With the doubts and despairs of this life!

Be not downcast and dejected, O my heart!
-Not even if fragrant sandalwood
Burns away in funeral pyres
And sweet flowers sicken and die
On the stony countenances of Gods:
For obscure indeed in this vision of life.
Let thy silvery laughter
Ring through all the riddles of this mortal span!

Be not downest and dejected, O my heart!
We see through a glass darkly,
And our values are uncertain.

But bewilderment is ever
The augury of knowledge.
Through the days of deluge
And of dreariness then,
Like the cuckoo, keep thou alive
The song of spring in thy breast!"

-Padmashree Kanhaiyalal Sethi

OPENING QUOTE

~~~~~~

"We want to lead mankind to the place where there is neither the Vedas, nor the Bible, nor the Koran; yet this has to be done by harmonizing the Vedas, the Bible and the Koran. Mankind ought to be taught that religions are but the varied expressions of the religion which is oneness."

-Swami Vivekananda

~~~~~~

DAWN

- Whosoever kills an innocent human being, it shall be as if has killed all mankind, and whosoever saves the life of one, it shall be as if he has saved the life of all mankind.

  -The Holy Quran

- There is no way to peace. Peace is the way.

  –M.K Gandhi

- Water and air, the two essential fluids; on which all life depends, have become global garbage cans.

  -Jacques Yves Cousteau

- The point is, there is no feasible excuse for what we are, for what we have made of ourselves. We have chosen to put profits before people, money before morality, dividends before decency, fanaticism before fairness and our own trivial comforts before the unspeakable agonies of others.

  -Iain Banks

- When a man is wrapped up in himself he makes a pretty small package.

  -John Rustin

- If the benevolent minded people could but visualise the agonies connected with the breeding, railing, transporting and slaughtering of the defenceless victims of human voracity, they would abhor the bloody morsel they now pick so daintily from their dinner plates.

  -Rev. Dr. Walter Walsh

- I've often said, the only thing standing between me and greatness is 'me'.

-Woody Allen

- The measure of intelligence is the ability to change.

-Albert Einstein

- My mother taught me as a boy.....'Ever to confess you're bored means you have no inner resources'.

-John Berryman

- We are made wise not by the recollection of our past, but by the responsibility of our future.

-George Bernard Shaw

- The habit of common and continuous speech is a symptom of mental deficiency. It proceeds from not knowing what is going on in other people's mind.

-Walter Bagehot

- Behaviour is a mirror in which everyone displays his image.

-The Gita

- When you are content to be simply yourself and don't compare or compete, everybody will respect you.

-Lao Tzu

- The hardest job kids face today is learning good manners without seeing any.

-Fred Astaire

- In my parents I saw a model where they were always communicating; doing things together. They were really kind of a team. I wanted some of that magic myself.

-Bill Gates

- The chains of habit are too weak to be felt until they are too strong to be broken.

-Dr Samuel Johnson

- Grief can take care of itself, but to get the full value from joy and happiness you must have somebody to share and divide it with.

-Mark Twain

- I have often thought upon death, and I find it the least of all evils.

-Francis Bacon

- Never lose sight of the fact that old age needs so little but needs that little so much.

-Margaret Will

- Luck to me is hard work and realising what is opportunity and what isn't.

-Lucile Ball

- Every form of addiction is bad, no matter whether the narcotic or alcohol or morphine or idealism.

-Carl Jung

- Anger begins with folly and ends with repentance.

-Henry George Bohn

- A promise made is a debt unpaid.

-Robert William Service

- We can only see a short distance ahead but we can see plenty there that needs to be done.

–Alan Turing

- Nothing happens to any man that he is not formed by nature to bear.

–Marcus Aurelius

- Success is how high you bounce when you hit bottom.

-General George Patton

- It can be said with some justification that things have become so bad not so much due to the wickedness of the bad as because of the apathy of the good.

–Anonymous

- 10% of the conflicts are due to difference in opinion. 90% are due to wrong tone of voice.

-Anonymous

- If a small thing has the power to make you angry, does that not indicate something about your size?

-Sydney J. Harris

- Worrying does not take away tomorrow's troubles; it takes away today's peace.

-Dale Carnegie

- How poor are they that have no patience: what wound did ever heal but by degrees?

-William Shakespeare

- If you want to achieve excellence, you can get there today. As of this second, quit doing less-than excellent work.

-Thomas J. Watson

- Our scientific power has outrun our spiritual power. We have guided missiles and misguided men.

-Martin Luther King

- To acquire the habit of reading is to construct for yourself a refuge from almost all the miseries of life.

-W. Somerset Maugham

- Dream does not become reality through magic. It takes sweat, determination and hard work.

-Colin Powell

- Enjoy yourself. It's later than you think.

–Anonymous

- There is no real excellence in all this world which can be separated from right living.

–Anonymous

- Your faith can move mountains, and your doubt can create them.

-Anonymous

- Sharing the pain and sufferings of others and the willingness to give something of one's own self, be it money, time or even plain concern, makes us uniquely human.

-Sudarshan Agarwal

- My concern is not whether God is on our side, my greatest concern is to be on God's side.

-Abraham Lincon

- What you do today can improve all your tomorrows.

-Ralph Marston

ॐ

"Happy, thrice happy, every one

Who sees his labor well begun,

And not perplexed and multiplied,

By idly waiting for time and tide!"

-Henry Wadsworth Longfellow

ॐ

VI
Experience

ॐ

[Translation: Courage in adversity,
Patience in prosperity,
Oratory in assembly,
Bravery in battle,
Modesty in fame,
Attachment to knowledge,
All these are naturally found in the great persons.]"

-unknown

ॐ

OPENING QUOTE

૭૪

~~~~~~

"If you would not be forgotten as soon as you are dead, write things worth reading or do things worth writing."

-Benjamin Franklin

~~~~~~

૭૪

EXPERIENCE

- Human beings, who are almost unique in having the ability to learn from the experience of others, are also remarkable for their apparent disinclination to do so.

-Douglas Adams

- Always remember that your present situation is not your final destination; the best is yet to come.

-Hilary Hinton Ziglar

- A happy family is but an earlier heaven.

-Sir John Bowring

- The greater our knowledge increases, the more our ignorance unfolds.

-John F. Kennedy

- The difficulty lies not so much in developing new ideas as in escaping from the old ones.

-J.M. Keynes

- Against criticism a man can neither protest nor defend himself; he must act in spite of it, and then it will gradually yield to him.

-Johann Wolfgang Von Goethe

- Maturity has more to do with the kind of experiences you've had, and what you've learned from them and less to do with how many birthdays you've celebrated.

–Anonymous

- The man who was not content to do small things well would leave great things undone.

-Ellen Glasgow

- It would be unsound fancy and self- contradictory to expect that things which have never yet been done can be done except by means which have never yet been tried.

-Francis Bacon

- Man has three ways of acting wisely. First, on meditation; that is the noblest. Secondly, on imitation; that is the easiest. Thirdly, on experience; that is the bitterest.

–Confucius

- Experience is a comb which nature gives to men when they are bald.

–Proverb

- Timely service, like timely gifts, is double in value.

-George Macdonald

- In a world where it is so easy to neglect, deny, pervert and suppress the truth, the scientist may find his discipline severe. For him, truth is seldom the sudden light that shows new order and beauty; more often, truth is the uncharted rock that sinks his ship in the dark.

-John Warcup Cornforth

- Better a lie that soothes than a truth that hurts.

-Czech Proverb

- Reason cannot prevail where reason cannot penetrate.

-Peter Quenelle

- I feel that one lies to oneself more than to anyone else.

-Lord Byron

- When you say that you agree to a thing in principle, you mean that you have not the slightest intention of carrying it out in practice.

-Otto Von Bismarck

- A dinner lubricates business.

-Lord Stowell

- When it is a question of money, everybody is of same religion.

–Voltaire

- Silence is one of the hardest arguments to refute.

-Josh Billings

- Many people fail in life, not for lack of ability or brains or even courage but simply because they have never organised their energies around a goal.

-Elbert Hubbard

- Those who attain any excellence commonly spend life in one pursuit; for excellence is not often granted upon easier terms.

-Dr Samuel Johnson

- A good plan is like a road map: it shows the final destination and usually the best way to get there.

-H. Stanley Judd

- No one can make you feel inferior without your consent.

-Eleanor Roosevelt

- The less one has to do, the less time one finds to do it.

-Lord Chesterfield

- It seldom pays to be rude. It never pays to be only half rude.

-Norman Douglas

- Laughter is much more important than applause. Applause is almost a duty. Laughter is a reward. Laughter means they trust and like you.

-Carol Channing

- The gem cannot be polished without friction, nor man perfected without trials.

–Confucius

- Whatever is begun in anger, ends in shame.

-Benjamin Franklin

- Learn to listen. Opportunity sometimes knocks very softly.

-Frank Tyger

- An army of sheep led by a lion would defeat an army of lions led by a sheep.

-Napoleon Bonaparte

- Hypocrisy is a tribute that vice pays to virtue.

-Francois de La Rochefoucauld

- Wandering re-establishes the original harmony which once existed between man and the universe.

-Anatole France

- Men of age object too much, consult too long, adventure too little.

-Dale Carnegie

- Experience is the extract of suffering.

-Arthur Helps

- If you can recognize illusion as illusion, it dissolves. The recognition of illusion is also its ending. Its survival depends on your mistaking it for reality.

-Eckhart Tolle

- Planning an over-crowded day causes tension and results in early fatigue. There should be some breathing space in switching over from one job to other. This also facilitates accommodating unexpected calls and emergencies.

-G.D Birla

- Entangling in too much details, lengthy enquires into trifles and involvement in wrong type of work or at wrong stage takes heavy roll of time with little gains in return.

–Anonymous

- Reading self-development-course books and acquiring diversified knowledge in spare moments and learning from the wisdom of others is like putting money in bank. Someday it yields a rich harvest.

–Anonymous

- He who is the most slow in making a promise is the most faithful in the performance of it.

-Jean Jacques Rousseau

- We don't see things as they are, we see them as we are.

-Anais Nin

- Great spirits have always encountered violent opposition from mediocre minds.

-Albert Einstein

- None can destroy iron, but its own rust can! Likewise, none can destroy a person but his own mindset can.

-Ratan Tata

- Man in general judge more from appearances than from reality. All men have eyes, but few have the gift of penetration.

-Niccolo Machiavelli

- After crosses and losses, men grow humbler and wiser.

-Benjamin Franklin

- Imagination is more important than knowledge.

-Albert Einstein

- The injury we do and the one we suffer are not weighed in the same scale.

-Aesop

- Worry a little bit every day and in a lifetime you will lose a couple of years. If something is wrong, fix it if you can. But train yourself not to worry; worry never fixes anything.

-Ernest Hemingway

- All religions have originated from god but in them lies a trace of the imperfection of man because they pass through the wisdom and language of man.

-M.K Gandhi

- Some of our important choices have a time limit. If we delay a decision, the opportunity is gone forever.

-James E Frust

- Experience is simply the name we give our mistakes.

-Oscar Wilde

ॐ

~~~~~~

"God and a soldier all people adore
In time of war, but not before;
And when war is over and all things are righted,
God is neglected and an old soldier slighted."

-Rudyard Kipling

~~~~~~

ॐ

VII
Faith

ॐ

"MY ASPIRATION

.

He who conquered love and hatred,
And vanquished sensual temptation,
True cosmic knowledge who attained,
And showed the path to salvation;

.

Some may call him Buddha, Hari, Jin,
Or may call him Brahma, Supreme;
His thoughts and deep devotion may
Be in my heart and mind and dream"

-Maitri

ॐ

OPENING QUOTE

৪৩

"*Asceticism doesn't lie in ascetic robes or in ashes. Asceticism doesn't lie in the earring or in the shaven head; nor does it lie in blowing a conch. Asceticism lies in remaining pure amidst impurities.*"

-Guru Nanak

৪৩

FAITH

- Right Faith (Samyak Darshana), Right Knowledge (Samyak Jnana) and Right Conduct (SamyakCharitra) are the ways to Moksha which is all bliss and the final liberation.

-Lord Mahavira

- I do not know any religion apart from human activity. The spiritual law does not work in a vacuum but in the ordinary activities of life. The religion which takes no account of practical affairs and does not help to solve them is no religion.

-M.K. Gandhi

- A Sannyasi cannot belong to any religion, for his is a life of independent thought, which draws from all religions; his is a life of realisation, not merely of theory or belief, much less of dogma.

-Swami Vivekananda

- Men never do evil so completely and cheerfully as when they do it from religious conviction.

-Blaise Pascal

- There is a church, a mosque, a temple, a synagogue in me. Yet, like a hoopoe trapped in the minaret of sacrifice, I long for your shrine.

-Moshin B. Mushtaq

- Philosophy, if it cannot answer so many questions as we could wish, has at least the power of asking questions which increase the interest of the world, and show the strangeness and wonder lying just below the surface even in the commonest things of daily life.

-Bertrand Russell

- Faith is the bird that sings when the dawn is still dark.

-Rabindranath Tagore

- Faith is a highly distinctive kind of knowledge, a knowledge that works through love... through the heart, and because we misunderstand the nature of this knowledge, we resist it or fail to respond fully to its mysterious call.

-James Arraj

- Faith is the highest passion in a human being. Many in every generation may not come that far, but none comes further.

-Soren Kierkegaard

- Doubt is a pain too lonely to know that faith is his twin brother.

-Kahlil Gibran

- We can live without religion and meditation. But we cannot survive without human affection.

-Dalai Lama

- If we could see miracle of a single flower clearly, our whole life would change.

-Gautama Buddha

- The human race has only two unlimited capacities; one for suffering and one for lying. I want to fight religion as the root of all human lying and the only excuse for human suffering.

-Ayn Rand

- Morality is like a shadow; religion is the real figure. When religion is there, morality comes on its own; it has to come.

–Anonymous

- Faith begins as an experiment and ends as an experience.

-Sir William Ralph Inge

- That what you really believe in always happens. And the belief in a thing makes it happen.

-Frank Lloyd Wright

- Education is the manifestation of perfection already in man and religion is the innermost core of education.

-Martin Tupper

- Absolute faith corrupts as absolutely as absolute power.

-Eric Hoffer

- Faith is the force of life.

-Count Leo Tolstoy

- My religion consists of a humble admiration of the illimitable superior spirit who reveals himself in the slight details we are not able to perceive with our frail and feeble mind.

-Albert Einstein

- So when you feel you are broken, be rest assured that God is planning to utilize you for something great.

–Anonymous

- God brings men into deep waters, not to drown them, but to cleanse them.

-John H. Aughey

- All great truths began as blasphemies.

-George Bernard Shaw

- Charity is the perfection and ornament of religion.

-Joseph Addison

- The truth of an upright man must be accepted on his own terms. Moreover, since natures vary, we must agree that all the beauties of human excellence may be fostered by faith that we do not share.

-Victor Hugo

- There lives more faith in honest doubt.

-Lord Tennyson

- The worst vice of a fanatic is his sincerity.

-Oscar Wilde

- Belief is the ignition switch that gets you off the launching pad.

-Denis Waitley

- Alone let him constantly meditate in solitude on that which is salutary for his soul, for he who meditates in solitude attains supreme bliss.

-Guru Nanak

- Anyone who thinks sitting in church can make you a Christian must also think that sitting in a garage can make you a car.

-Garrison Keillor

- So that, in effect, religion, which should most distinguish us from beasts, and ought most peculiarly , to delete as rational creatures, above brutes, is that wherein men often appear most irrational, and more senseless than beasts themselves.

-John Locke

- Do the duty, that is best, leave unto the Lord the rest.

–Morituri Salutamus

ॐ

"Useless are your pilgrimages galore
If your thoughts remain as before
And useless is a whole month's fast
If your mind continues its merry repast.

Of what use is your sacrificial fire
If it doesn't burn your base desire
And God will surely set your prayers aside
If you visit a temple and then show pride."

-Kabir

ॐ

VIII
Fragrance

"INVICTUS

Out of the night that covers me,
Black as the pit from pole to pole,
I thank whatever gods may be
For my unconquerable soul.

In the fell clutch of circumstance
I have not winced nor cried aloud.
Under the bludgeonings of chance
My head is bloody, but unbowed.

Beyond this place of wrath and tears
Looms but the horror of the shade,
And yet the menace of the years
Finds, and shall find, me unafraid.

It matters not how strait the gate,
How charged with punishments the scroll,
I am the master of my fate,
I am the captain of my soul."

-William Ernest Henley

OPENING QUOTE

~~~~~~

"India is the cradle of the human race, birthplace of human speech, mother of history, the grandmother of legend and the great grandmother of tradition. Our most valuable and most instructive materials in the history of man are treasured up in India."

-Mark Twain

~~~~~~

FRAGRANCE

- The work of an unknown good man is like a vein of water flowing underground, secretly making the ground greener.

  –Thomas Carlyle

- Am I not destroying my enemies when I make friends of them?

  -Abraham Lincoln

- A man may fall many times, but he won't be a failure until he says that someone pushed him.

  -Elmer G. Letterman

- Man's unhappiness, as I construe, comes of his greatness; it is because there is an infinite in him, which with all his cunning, he cannot quite bury under the finite.

  -Thomas Carlyle

- Truth is tough. It will not break like a bubble, at a touch; nay, you may kick it about all day like a football, and it will be round and full at evening.

  -Oliver Wendell Holmes

- A man may die, nations may rise and fall, but an idea lives on. Ideas have endurance without death.

  -Johann Wolfgang Von Goethe

- You have achieved success in your field when you do not know whether what you are doing is work or play.

-Warren Beatty

- Resentment is like taking poison and hoping the other person dies.

-St. Augustine

- One can survive everything, nowadays, except death, and live down everything except a good reputation.

-Oscar Wilde

- The secret of happiness is to make others believe that they are the cause of it.

-Al Batt

- Where the willingness is great, the difficulties cannot be great.

-Niccolo Machiavelli

- The world may call us weak, but we must not weaken our ideal.

-M.K. Gandhi

- Excellence is doing ordinary things extraordinarily well.

-Jose Ortega Y. Gasset

- The world would be a different place if it's victors, in wars and elections, understood that sometimes one needs to lose.

-The Telegraph, 20th April, 2003

- A single day is enough to make us a little larger.

-Paul Klee

- We should all be concerned about the future because we will have to spend the rest of our lives there.

-Charles F. Kettering

- The thing I hate about an argument is that it always interrupts a discussion.

-Gilbert Keith Chesterton

- Remember not only to say the right thing in the right place, but far more difficult still, to leave unsaid the wrong thing at the tempting moment.

-Benjamin Franklin

- The full use of today is the best preparation for tomorrow.

–Anonymous

- Better than a gift given with a joyous heart, are sweet words spoken with a cheerful smile.

-The Tirukkural

- You never get a second chance to make a first impression.

-Will Rogers

- If the only prayer you said in your whole life was – 'THANK YOU' that would suffice.

-Meister Eckhart

- The best sleeping pill is a clear conscience.

–Anonymous

- Happiness is in the sight of a sleeping child.

–Anonymous

- Dream is not what you see in sleep. Dream is the thing which does not let you sleep.

-Dr A.P.J Abdul Kalam

- It is all dark; stark dark, but nobody forbids you from lighting a lamp.

-Acharya Mahashraman

- Peace rules the day where reason rules the mind.

–Anonymous

- The fellow who does things that count, doesn't usually stop to count them.

-Albert Einstein

- What you leave behind is not what is engraved in stone monuments, but what is woven into the lives of others.

–Pericles

- As the purse is emptied the heart is filled.

-Victor Hugo

- What sculpture is to a block of marble, education is to the soul.

-Joseph Addison

- He is happiest, be he king or peasant, who finds peace in his home.

-Johann Wolfgang Von Goethe

- Politeness is good nature regulated by good sense.

-Sydney Smith

- In the pursuit of happiness, half the world is on the wrong scent. They think it consists in having and getting, and in being served by others. Happiness is really found in giving and in serving others.

-Henry Drummond

- The life given to us by nature is short, but the memory of a well- spent life is eternal.

-Marcus Tullius Cicero

- If its not a beautiful morning, let your cheerfulness make it one.

-H. Jackson Brown Jr

- If we have no peace, it is because we have forgotten that we belong to each other.

-Mother Teresa

- Be modest. A lot was accomplished before you were born.

-Anonymous

- A flower's appeal is in its contradictions- so delicate in form yet strong in fragrance. So small in size yet big in beauty. So short in life yet long in effect.

-Adabella Radici

- One may contribute... to the beauty of things by making one's own life and environment beautiful, so far as one's power reaches. This includes moral beauty, one of the qualities of humanity.

-R. Jeffers

- Whoever you are, bear in mind that appearance is not reality. So the next time you see a person with a composed face and a soft voice, remember that inside her mind she might be solving an equation, composing a sonnet, designing a hat. She might, that is, be deploying the powers of quiet.

-Susan Cain

- It is not for him to pride himself who loveth his own country, but rather for him who loveth the whole world. The earth is but one country and mankind its citizens.

–Bahaullah

- Love the giver more than the gift.

-Brigham Young

- An honest man is always a child.

-Socrates

༖

"No work so great
But what admits decay,
No act so glorious
But must fade away...

Old things must yield to new,
Common to strange,
Perpetual motion brings
Perpetual change."

-James Miller

IX
Galaxy

ॐ

"**ETERNAL WILL**

All speaks of change: the renovated forms
Of long forgotten things arise again;
The light of suns, the breath of angry storms,
The everlasting motions of the main.

These are but engines of the eternal will,
The One intelligence, whose potent sway
Has ever acted, and is acting still
While stars, and worlds and systems all obey."

-Humphry Davy

ॐ

OPENING QUOTE

ജ

~~~~~~

"Learn to distinguish the difference between errors of knowledge and breaches of morality. An error of knowledge is not a moral flaw, provided you are willing to correct it; only a mystic would judge human beings by the standard of an impossible, automatic omniscience. But a breach of morality is the conscious choice of an action you know to be evil, or a wilful evasion of knowledge, a suspension of sight and thought."

-Ayn Rand

~~~~~~

ജ

GALAXY

- Tact is the art of making a point without making an enemy.

-Isaac Newton

- Pause before judging, pause before assuming, pause before accusing. Pause whenever you are about to reach harshly and you will avoid doing and saying things you will later regret.

-Lord Deschene

- Never forget two people in your life. The person who lost everything just to make you win-Your FATHER and the person who was with you in every pain-YOUR MOTHER.

-Anonymous

- Sometimes we struggle with a tasteless coffee, till the last sip and then we find sugar lying at the bottom. That is life, sweetened but not stirred well.

-Anonymous

- Do the best you can until you know better, then when you know better, do better.

-Maya Angelou

- True heroism is remarkably sober, very undramatic. It is not the urge to surpass all others at whatever cost, but the urge to serve others at whatever cost.

-Arthur Ashe

- I find I am much prouder of the victory I obtain over myself, when, in the very ardour of dispute, I make myself submit to my adversary's force of reason.

-Michel De Montaigue

- The object of opening the mind, as of opening the mouth, is to shut it again on something solid.

-GK Chesterton

- Failure to summon forth the courage to risk a nondogmatic and nonevasive stance on crucial existential matters can blur our ethical vision.

-Stephen Batchelor

- Make yourself so good that the good feels great with you.

-Anonymous

- The tragedy of life is not that it ends so soon, but that we wait so long to begin it.

-W.M Lewis

- It is fair, even handed, noble adjustment of things, that while there is infection in disease and sorrow, there is nothing in the world so irresistibly contagious as laughter and good humour.

-Charles Dickens

- No pessimist ever discovered the secret of the stars, or sailed to an uncharted land, or opened a new doorway for the human spirit. Life is either a great adventure or nothing.

-Helen Keller

- Labels like Indian or woman or Muslims.. are not more than starting points. No one can deny the persisting continuities of long traditions, sustained habitations, national language...but there seems no reason except fear and prejudice to keep insisting on their separation and distinctiveness, as if that was all human life was about.

-Edward Said

· As human beings, our greatness lies not so much in being able to remake the world as in being able to remake ourselves.

-Mahatma Gandhi

· Religion is part of our cultural and intellectual history. It was our first attempt at ...making sense of where we are in the universe and our first attempt at philosophy.

-Christopher Hitchens

· A good character is the best tombstone. Carve your name on hearts, not on marble.

-Charles Spurgeon

· Happiness comes from knowing that you are growing and helping others to grow.

-Anonymous

· God has been very good to me, for I never dwell upon anything wrong which a person has done, so as to remember it afterwards. If I do remember it, I always see some other virtue in that person.

-St. Teresa of Avila

· I came into the world charged with the duty to uphold the right in every place, to destroy sin and evil.. the only reason I took birth was to see that righteousness may flourish, that good may live, and tyrants be torn out by their roots.

-Guru Gobind Singh

- Good relationships are like trees. They demand attention and care in the beginning, but once they blossom, they provide you shade in all situations of life.

-Anonymous

- Adopt this art in your life. If the fight is with your own people, learn to lose it.

-Anonymous

- Successful people have two things on their lips--Smile to solve the problem and silence to avoid the problem.

-Anonymous

- Speak in such a way that others love to listen to you. Listen in such a way that others love to speak to you.

-Anonymous

- People are garbage, full of disappointment and anger. You just wave, smile, wish them and move on. You love those who treat you right, pray for those who treat you wrong. Life is 10% how you make it and 90% how you take it.

-Anonymous

- Relationships never die a natural death; they are always murdered by ego, bad attitude, ill behaviour, hidden benefits or ignorance.

-Anonymous

- Talent and looks are God given, be thankful. Fame and money are man created, be grateful. Attitude and ego are self created, be careful.

-Anonymous

- If you go to heaven without being naturally qualified for it, you will not enjoy yourself there.

-Anonymous

- The best revenge is massive success.

-Frank Sinatara

- Whenever science makes a discovery, the devil grabs it while the angels are debating the best way to use it.

-A Valentine

- A word of encouragement during a failure is worth more than an hour of praise after success.

-Anonymous

- Learning is a treasure that will follow its owner everywhere.

-Anonymous

- Nothing can dim the light that shines within.

-Maya Angelou

- You come to love not by finding the perfect person but by seeing an imperfect person perfectly.

-Sam Keen

- Knowledge speaks, but wisdom listens.

-Jimi Hendrix

· Success usually comes to those who are too busy to be looking for it.

-Henry David Thoreau

છ

~~~~~~

"*Let someone call me good or bad*
Let riches come or turn away
Whether I live for million years
Or I face death this very day.

.

Whether someone does frighten me
Or even tempt me in some way
May my steps never falter
From proven good and righteous way."

-unknown

~~~~~~

છ

X
Honey Dips

ಬಂ

"THE WORM
Turn, turn thy hasty foot aside,
Nor crush that helpless worm!
The frame thy scornful thoughts deride
From God thy received its form.

The common lord of all that move,
From whom thy being flowed,
A portion of his boundless love
On that poor worm bestowed.

The sun, the moon, the stars he made
To all his creatures free;
And spread over earth the grassy blade,
For worms as well as thee.

Let them enjoy their little day,
The humble bliss they receive;
Oh, do not, lightly take away
The life which thou can't give!"

-Thomas Gisborne

OPENING QUOTE

ॐ

~~~~~~

"Gaining mastery over our destructive propensities through the exercise of awareness and self-discipline at the levels of body, speech and mind frees us from inner turmoil that naturally arises when our behaviour is at odds with our ideals."

-The XIII Dalai Lama

~~~~~~

ॐ

HONEY DIPS

• 83 •

• Let the refining and improving of your own life keep you so busy that you have little time to criticize others.

-Anonymous

• The longer I live the more I am convinced that the one thing worth living for and dying for is the privilege of making someone more happy and more useful. A man who never does anything to lift his fellows ever makes a sacrifice.

-Booker T. Washington

• Harmony makes small things grow, lack of it makes great things decay.

–Sallust

• 'Hatred is always a sin,' my mother told me, 'Remember that one drop of hatred in your soul will spread and discolour everything like a drop of black ink in white milk.' I was struck by that and meant to try it, but knew I shouldn't waste the milk.

-Alice Munro

• Knowledge of physical science will not console me for ignorance of morality in time of affection, but knowledge of morality will always console me for Ignorance of physical science.

-Blaze Pascal

• A man draws nearer to the stars, why should he not also draw nearer to his neighbour?

-Lyndon Baines Johnson

· Silence becomes cowardice when occasion demands speaking out the whole truth and acting accordingly.

-M.K. Gandhi

· Adopt the pace of nature: her secret is patience.

-Ralph Waldo Emerson

· There is no duty we so much underrate as the duty of being happy.

-Robert Louis Stevenson

· It is often better not to see an insult than to avenge it.

–Seneca

· As one lamp lights another it does not glow less, so nobleness enriches nobleness.

-James Russell Lowell

· I thought myself badly off because I had no boots, until I went out and saw a man who had no legs.

-Anonymous

· Prosperity is only an instrument to be used, not a deity to be worshipped.

-John Calvin Coolidge

· Fame is something which must be won; honour is something which must not be lost.

-Arthur Schopenhauer

- Teach us to number our days and recognize how few they are; help us to spend them as we should.

-Psalm

- I recommend you to take care of the minutes; for hours will take care of themselves.

-Lord Chesterfield

- I never make the mistake of arguing with people for whose opinions I have no respect.

-Edward Gibbon

- The main things which seem to me important on their own account, and not merely as means to other things, are knowledge, art, instinctive happiness and relations of friendship or affection.

-Bertrand Russell

- I count him braver who overcomes his desires than one who conquers his enemies, for the hardest victory is over self.

-Aristotle

- Too many people are looking for the right person, instead of being the right person.

-Corrina Bunch

- For every minute you're angry, you lose sixty seconds of happiness.

-Ralph Waldo Emerson

- The mode of living which is founded upon a total harmlessness towards all creatures.... Is the highest morality.

- The Mahabharata

- Listen a hundred times, ponder a thousand times, speak once!

-Anonymous

- The best way to cheer yourself up is to try to cheer somebody else up.

-Mark Twain

- The tears in others eyes should be for us not due to us.

-Mother Teresa

- It pays to know the enemy--not least because at some time you may have the opportunity to turn him into a friend.

-Margret Thatcher

- Greater than being great is being grateful.

–Anonymous

- Happiness is spending time with your grandparents.

-Anonymous

- Be kind, be decent, be generous, be tolerant, compassionate and understanding. Be fast to praise, slow to judge.

-Allen Drury

- One is happy as a result of one's own efforts, once one knows the necessary ingredients of happiness--simple tastes, a certain degree of courage, self-denial to a point, love of work and above all, a clear conscience.

-George Sand

- And in the end, it is not the years in your life, but the life in your years that counts.

-Abraham Lincoln

- Mind is not a dustbin to keep anger, hatred and jealousy.

-Diogenes

- If you've grown up without naturally happy disposition, it is not too late to cultivate one.

-John A. Schindler

- The soul that perpetually overflows with kindness and sympathy, will always be cheerful.

-Parke Godwon

- Honour women! They entwine and weave heavenly roses in our earthly life.

-Friedrich Schiller

- Punctuality means moving in harmony with the steps of time. Time does not remain in good company of those who cannot keep appointments or too often fail to maintain schedules.

-Acharya Tulsi

- The best way of spending spare time is to devote it to certain works of art or beauty or usefulness so that one satisfies not only his creative urge but also produces something of value to the society.

-Anonymous

- Recommend to your children virtue; that alone can make them happy; not gold.

-Ludwig Van Beethoven

- Learning never exhausts the mind.

-Leonardo Da Vinci

- I earn that I eat, get that I wear, owe no man hate, envy no man's happiness; glad of other men's good, content with my harm.

-William Shakespeare

- The first great gift and the best inheritance we can bestow on our children is a good example. A good example is the best sermon.

-Thomas Morell

- If a man aims to move the world, he must first move himself.

–Socrates

- Show respect even to people who don't deserve it; not as a reflection of their character, but as a reflection of yours.

-Dave Willis

- The only good is knowledge, and the only evil is ignorance.

–Diogenes

Peace hath her victories, no less renowned than war.

-John Milton

- How few our real wants, and how vast our imaginary ones.

-Johann KasparLavater

- You cannot change your future but you can change your habits and surely your habits will change your future.

-Dr A.P.J Abdul Kalam

- There is no greater wealth than wisdom; no greater poverty than ignorance; no greater heritage than culture.

-Nahjul Balagha

- Become the kind of a person who brightens a room just by entering it.

-H. Jackson Brown Jr

- He that is good for making excuses is seldom good for anything else.

-Benjamin Franklin

- God enjoins you to treat women well, for they are your mothers, sisters and aunts.

-Prophet Mohammad

ॐ

~~~~~~

"*A WISE OLD OWL*

.

A wise old owl sat on an oak,
The more he sat the less he spoke!
The less he spoke the more he heard!
Why aren't we like that wise old bird?"

-EH Richards

~~~~~~

ॐ

Insight

> **"I SIT AND LOOK OUT**
> *I sit and look out upon all the sorrows of the world*
> *And upon all oppression and shame;*
> *I hear secret convulsive sobs from young men,*
> *At anguish with themselves, remorseful after deeds done;*
>
> *I see, In low life, the mother misused by her children, dying,*
> *Neglected, gaunt, desperate;*
> *I see the wife misused by her husband,*
> *I see the treacherous seducer of young women;*
>
> *I mark the rankings of jealousy and unrequited love,*
> *Attempted to be hid – I see these sights on the earth;*
> *I see the workings of battle, pestilence, tyranny,*
> *I see martyrs and prisoners;*
>
> *I observe a famine at sea – I observe the sailors casting lots*
> *Who shall be kill'd, to preserve the lives of the rest;*
> *I observe the slights and degradations cast by arrogant persons*
> *Upon labourers, the poor, and upon negroes, and the like;*
> *All these – all the meanness and agony without end,*
> *I sitting, look out upon, See, hear, and am silent."*

-Walt Whitman

OPENING QUOTE

~~~~~~

*"A gardener, while gardening with love, identities with the
Vegetable kingdoms. Through gardening he attains oneness With
the whole universe.
That way gardening become a noble act, a
Prayer and a play -all life is a play; a divine drama.........
We should performer actions as naturally as a bird sings."*

-Vinoba Bhave

~~~~~~

INSIGHT

- Non-violence is the first article of my faith; it is also the last article of my creed.

  -M.K. Gandhi

- Nice words written on a balloon which was flying high up in the sky..." it is not what's outside, but what's inside, that takes you to the top."

  -Anonymous

- When making a decision of minor importance, I have always found it advantageous to consider all the pros and cons. In vital matters. Such as the choice of mate or a profession, the decision should come from the unconscious, from somewhere within ourselves.

  -Sigmund Freud

- We can form a precise idea of order, but not of disorder. Beauty, virtue, happiness, all have their proportions; ugliness, vice and unhappiness have none.

  -Jacques-Henri Bernardin De Saint-Pierre

- Unlawful pleasure, trenching on another's rights, is delusive and envenomed pleasure – its hollowness disappoints at the time, its poison cruelly tortures afterwards, its effects deprave forever.

  -Charlotte Bronte

- Whatever an enemy may do to an enemy, whatever a hater may do to a hater, the harm caused by a misdirected mind is even greater still.

  -The Dhammapada

- Authority and responsibility are like the bow and arrow, the hammer and the nail, rain and sunshine, each useless without the other.

–Chanakya

- Most people enter into relationships with an eye towards what they can get out of them, rather than what they can put into them

-Neale Donald Walsch

- If it turns out that there is a God....the worst that you can say about him is that basically he's an under-achiever.

-Woody Allen

- I see two initial motives in man's inner life: the search for meaning and the search for eternal.

-Nikolai Berdyaev

- Earth and sky, woods and fields, lakes and rivers, the mountain and the sea are excellent school-masters and teach some of us more that we can ever learn from books.

-Sir John Lubbock

- The greatest truths are simplest, and so are the greatest men.

-Vinoba Bhave

- Wherever you are is the entry point.

–Kabir

- As long as men massacre animals, they will kill each other. Indeed, he who sows the seeds of murder and pain cannot reap joy and love.

–Pythagoras

- The cradle rocks above an abyss, and common sense tells us that our existence is but a brief crack of light between two eternities of darkness.

-Vladimir Nabokov

- Never let success hide its emptiness from you; achievement its nothingness; toil its desolation. Keep alive the incentive to push on further, that pain in the soul drives us beyond ourselves.

-Dag Hammarskjold

- A reputation once broken may possibly be repaired, but the world will always keep their eyes on the spot where the crack was.

-Joseph Hall

- Men are rewarded and punished not for what they do, but rather for how their acts are defined. This is why men are more interested in better justifying themselves than in better behaving themselves.

-Thomas Stephen Szasz

- I would rather live my life as if there is a God and die to find out there isn't, than live my life as if there isn't and die to find out there is.

-Albert Camus

- Men see objects, women see the relationship between objects....it is an extra dimension of feeling which we men are without and one that makes war abhorrent to all real women.

-John Fowles

- Sit for a while and relax. Leave this turmoil for while. Leave all ambition for a little while. Leave the mind's running around, leave its rat race. Simply sit a while and sink into yourself. A light will gradually begin spreading inside you.

-Acharya Mahapragya

- All our knowledge brings us nearer to our ignorance.

-Thomas Stearns Eliot

- Half my life is an act of revision.

-John Irvin

- Touch, taste, sight, smell and hearing are the senses. He who controls these five magically controls the world.

-RamkrishnaParamhansa

- Don't tell yourself to practice virtue tomorrow, do it now , for it will be your deathless companion when you die.

-The Tirukkural

- Knowledge of the self leads to the knowledge of the difference between good and evil.

–Socrates

- You have to grow from the inside out. None can teach you, none can make you spiritual. There is no other teacher, but your own soul.

-Swami Vivekananda

- Reforms must come from within, not from without. You cannot legislate for virtue.

-James Cardinal Gibbons

- A word spoken in wrath is the sharpest sword; covetousness is the deadliest poison; passion is the fiercest fire; ignorance is the darkest night.

-Gautam Buddha

- Learn to be a witness in ordinary life.

-The Gita

- If I don't have time to live my life well the first time, when am I going to find the time to go back and live it over?

-Robert Fulham

- The mind is like a sheet of white paper. The impressions it receives the most often and retains the longest are black ones.

-J.C Hare

- The best way to succeed in life is to act on advice you give to others.

–Anonymous

- Man is the only creature that refuses to be what he is.

-Albert Camus

- The good, the admirable reader identifies himself not with the boy or the girl in the book, but with the mind that conceived and composed that book.

-Vladimir Nabokov

- For a seed to achieve its greatest expression, it must come completely undone. The shell cracks, its insides come out and everything changes. To someone who doesn't understand growth, it would look like complete destruction.

-Cynthia Occelli

- Justice is always violent to the party offending, for every man is innocent in his own eyes.

-Daniel Decos

- There's a victory, and defeat; the first and best of victories, the lowest and worst of defeats which each man gains or sustains at the hands not of another, but of himself.

–Plato

- Above all, don't lie to yourself. The man who lies to himself and listens to his own lies comes to such a pass that he cannot distinguish the truth within him, or around him, and so loses all respect.

-Fyodor Dostoevsky

- Success is the sum of small efforts - repeated day in and day out.

-Robert Collier

- It is true that man is no longer an animal, but is it also true that man has to become human? Being an animal is an event in the past, but to be human is still only a possibility in the future. We are in the middle and this is our pain.

-Osho

"The assumption that animals are without rights and the illusion that our treatment of them has no moral significance is a positively outrageous example of crudity and barbarity. Universal compassion is the only guarantee of morality."

-Arthur Schopenhauer

XII
Inspiration

"*Jo Hua Na Ab Tak Shabdbaddh*
Wah Ankanth Mera Kath Hoga
Aage Na Kisike Charan-Chinha
Wah Mere Pat Ka Ath Hoga

.

[<u>Translation</u>: What has not been woven into words yet
I will say only that unsaid
Where there are no foot-prints any further
My journey will start from that path untread.]"

-Kanhaiya Lal Sethiya

OPENING QUOTE

ॐ

"A hundred times every day I remind myself that my inner and outer life depended on the labours of other men, living and dead, and that I must exert myself in order to give in the same measure as I have received and am still receiving."

-Albert Einstein

ॐ

INSPIRATION

- A race horse that consistently runs just a second faster than another horse is worth millions of dollars more. Be willing to give that extra effort that separates the winner from the one in second place.

  -Marv A Collins

- Try to be a rainbow in someone's cloud.

  –Maya Angelon

- I am thankful to all those who said 'No'. Because of them, I did it myself.

  -Albert Einstein

- We are not permitted to choose the frame of our destiny. But what we put into it is ours.

  -Dag Hammarskjold

- The future belongs to those who see possibilities before they become obvious.

  -John Sculley

- The dogmas of the quiet past are inadequate to the stormy present. The occasion is piled high with difficulty, and we must rise with the occasion.

  -Abraham Lincoln

- Expect trouble as an inevitable part of life and when it comes, hold your head high, look it squarely in the eye and say, " I will be bigger than you. You cannot defeat me."

-Ann Landers

- If you have knowledge, let others light their candles at it.

-Margaret Fuller

- I want to see you shoot the way you shout.

-Theodore Roosevelt

- Discovery consists of seeing what everybody has seen and thinking what nobody has thought.

-Albert Szent Gyorgyi

- Always set a high value on spontaneous kindness.

-Dr Samuel Johnson

- The superior man is modest in his speech, but excels in his actions.

–Confucius

- Our greatest glory is not in never failing, but in rising up every time we fail.

-Ralph Waldo Emerson

- Success seems to be largely a matter of hanging on after others have let go.

-William Feather

- The test of a first-rate intelligence is the ability to hold two opposed ideas in mind at the same time and still retain the ability to function.

-F. Scott Fitzgerald

- Think like a man of action, act like a man of thought.

-Henri Bergson

- There is no passion to be found playing small- in settling for a life that is less than the one you are capable of living.

-Nelson Mandela

- Nothing is impossible, really. Start by doing what's necessary; then do what's possible; and suddenly you are doing the impossible.

-St Francis of Assisi

- Practice writing like running, the more you do it, the better you get at it.

-Natalie Goldberg

- We may feel that what we are doing is just a drop in the ocean. But the ocean would be less because of that missing drop.

-Mother Teresa

- To be yourself in a world that is constantly trying to make you something else is the greatest accomplishment.

-Ralph Waldo Emerson

- Forces against us can never be more powerful than the sources within us.

-Voltaire

- Impossible is a word only to be found in the dictionary of fools.

-Napoleon Bonaparte

- I really had a lot of dreams when I was a kid and I think a great deal of that grew out of the fact that I had a chance to read a lot.

-Bill Gates

- Hold up your head! You were not made for failure, you were made for victory. Go forward with a joyful confidence.

-George Eliot

- If you fail, never give-up because F.A.I.L means 'First Attempt In Learning'. End is not the End. In fact, E.N.D means "Effort Never Dies". If you get 'NO' as an answer, remember N.O means "Next Opportunity". So let us be positive.

-Dr A.P.J Abdul Kalam

- There is no greater delight than to be conscious of sincerity on self-examination.

–Mencius

- We cannot always build the future for our youth, but we can build our youth for the future.

-Franklin D. Roosevelt

- Curiosity is one of the permanent and certain characteristics of a vigorous intellect.

-Samuel Johnson

- The man who does not read good books has no advantage over the man who can't read.

-Mark Twain

- Never let the odds keep you from pursuing what you know in your heart you were meant to do.

-H. Jackson Brown Jr

- There is nothing noble in being superior to your fellow man; true nobility is being superior to your former self.

-Ernest Hemingway

- Don't let anyone say- "you can't do it."

-John ILhan

- Perfection is not attainable, but if we chase perfection we can catch excellence.

-Vince Lombardi

- Talk happiness. The world is sad enough without your woe. No path is wholly rough.

-Ella Wheeler Wilcox

- Instead of being concerned that you are not known, seek to be worthy of being known.

–Confucius

- Respect and praise is never asked, you have to earn it.

–Anonymous

- Reverence for life affords me my fundamental principle that good consists in maintaining, assisting and enhancing life, and that to destroy, to harm or to hinder life is evil.

-Albert Schweitzer

- I can, therefore I am.

-Simone Weil

൭

~~~~~~

"How doth the busy little bee
Improve each shining hour
And gather honey all day
From every opening flower."

-Issac Watts

~~~~~~

൭

XIII
Life

“*What is this life if full of care,*
We have no time to stand and stare?

No time to stand beneath the boughs
And stare as long as sheep or cows.

No time to see, when woods we pass,
Where squirrels hide their nuts in grass.

No time to see, in broad daylight,
Streams full of stars, like skies at night.

No time to turn at beauty's glance,
And watch her feet, how they can dance.

No time to wait till her mouth can
Enrich that smile her eyes began.

A poor life this if full of care,
We have no time to stand and stare.”

-W.H. Davies

OPENING QUOTE

ఐ

~~~~~~

- THE DALAI LAMA, WHEN ASKED WHAT SURPRISED HIM MOST ABOUT HUMANITY, ANSWERED,

> *"Man! Because he sacrifices his health in order to make money. Then he sacrifices money to recuperate his health and then he is so anxious about the future that he does not enjoy the present. The result being that he does not live in the present or the future; he lives as if he is never going to die, and then dies having never really lived."*

-from public records of Dalai Lama

~~~~~~

ఐ

LIFE

- We are swift to chide and slow to bless.....words of flattery fall in torrents from our lips but our tongue is chained when a short word of praise is due.

-The Bible

- The two most important days in your life are the days you are born and the day you find out why.

-Mark Twain

- In the last analysis, it is our conception of death which decodes our answers to all the questions that life puts to us.

-Dag Hammarskjold

- There are decades when nothing happens; and there are weeks where decades happen.

-Vladimir ILyich Lenin

- The test of a man is how much he can bear, how much he can share, how soon he can confess a mistake and how soon he can make amends for it.

-Prabha Gupta

- Society is indeed a contract.....it becomes a partnership not only between whose who are living, but also between those who are dead and those who are to be born.

-Edmund Burke

- The mode of living which is founded upon total harmlessness towards all creatures is the highest morality.

-Shantiparva

- Beginning today, treat everyone you meet as if they were going to be dead by midnight. Extend to them all the care, kindness and understanding you can muster, and do it with no thought of any reward. Your life will never be the same again.

-OgMandino

- The only disability in life is a bad attitude.

-Scott Hamilton

- When everyone is happy with you, then surely you have made many compromises in your life. When you are happy with everyone, surely you have ignored many faults of others.

–Anonymous

- No one knows about your integrity, your sincerity, your talent, your goodness unless you give out samples in action.

-Dr Sarvapalli Radhakrishnan

- Coincidence is God's way of remaining anonymous

-Albert Einstein.

- One of the mistakes man makes is the tendency to worry about things that cannot be changed or corrected.

-Marcus Tullius Cicero

- Life is a mirror; if you frown at it, it frowns back; if you smile, it returns the greetings.

-William Makepeace Thackeray

- Victory has hundred fathers, but defeat is an orphan.

-Galeazzo Ciano

- Virtue has never been as respectable as money.

-Mark Twain

- Those who know the least obey the best.

-George Farquhar

- We never know the worth of water till the well is dry.

-English Proverb

- I was never more hated than when I tried to be honest...on the other hand, I've never been more loved and appreciated than when I tried to "justify" and affirm someone's mistaken beliefs; or when I've tried to give my friends the incorrect, absurd answers they wished to hear.

-Ralph Waldo Emerson

- Change is the law of life. And those who look only to the past or present are certain to miss the future.

-John F. Kennedy

- When we choose to slow down and really experience the qualities of our lives, we get a whole new perspective on what living is all about.

-Herbert George Wells

- To the world you might be one person, but to one person you might be the world.

-Bill Wilson

- Many of life's failures are people who did not realize how close they were to success when they gave up.

  -Thomas Alva Edison

- Only your real friends will tell when your face is dirty.

  –Proverb

- Every day we slaughter our finest impulses.... A man, when he gets quiet, when he becomes desperately honest with himself, is capable of uttering profound truths.

  -Henry Miller

- The first forty years of life gives us the text; the next thirty supply the commentary on it.

  -Arthur Schopenhauer

- Our age of Anxiety is in great part the result of trying to do today's job with yesterday's tools and yesterday's concepts.

  -Marshall Mcluhan

- It is never too late to be what you might have been.

  -George Elliot

- Sometimes the best thing a mother can do for her children is not have another.

  -Mellinda Gates

ॐ

~~~~~~

"The thing that goes the farthest towards making a life worthwhile
That cost the least,and does the most, is just a pleasant smile.
It is full of worth and goodness too, with manly kindness blent
It's worth a million dollars and it doesn't cost a cent."

-Wilbur D. Nesbit

~~~~~~

ॐ

XIV
Merry Go Round

"HAPPY NEW YEAR
Free from the vanities of the world
Free from our follies absurd,
Free from the quirks of life
Free from ignoble strife,
Free from worry, free from fear
A happy new year to you, my dear.

Free from the dry tap, free from the power cut
Free from a leader's vows, free from a policeman's butt,
Free from the officer's pretence,
Free from hunger, free from tear
A happy new year to you, my dear.

Free from insensitive laws, free from inflated bill
Free from swollen eye, free from the sleeping pill,
Free from a made-up face, free from the mad, mad race
Full of bounty, full of grace,
Of sunny days and nights clear
A happy new year to you, my dear."

-Anonymous

OPENING QUOTE

☙

~~~~~~

"The world is like a board with holes in it and the square men have got into the round holes and the round into the square."

-Bishop Berkeley

~~~~~~

☙

MERRY GO ROUND

- An unalterable and unquestioned law of the musical world required that the German text of French operas sung by Swedish artists should be translated into Italian for the clearer understanding of English speaking audiences.

  -Edith Wharton

- A conference is a gathering of important people who singly can do nothing, but together can decide that nothing can be done.

  -Fred Allen

- Examinations are formidable even to the best prepared, for the greatest fool may ask more than the wisest man can answer.

  -Charles Caleb Colton

- The brain is a wonderful organ; it starts working the moment you get up in the morning and doesn't stop until you get into the office.

  -Robert Frost

- The capacity of human beings to bore one another seems to be vastly greater than that of any other animal. Some of their most esteemed inventions have no other apparent purpose – the dinner party for more than two, the epic poem, and the science of metaphysics.

  -Henry Louis Mencken

- The calmest husband makes the stormiest wife.

  -Isaac D'Israeli

- I sit on a man's back, choking him and making him carry me, and yet assure myself and others that I am very sorry for him and wish to ease his lot by all possible means – except by getting off his back.

-Count Leo Tolstoy

- Love is the dawn of marriage and marriage is the sunset of love.

-De Finod

- Usually we praise only to be praised.

-Francois de La Rochefoucauld

- City life: millions of people being lonesome together.

-Henry David Thoreau

- Women's weapons – water drops.

-William Shakespeare

- Nothing flatters a man as much as the happiness of his wife; he is always proud of himself as the source of it.

-Dr Samuel Johnson

- By all means marry: if you get a good wife you will be happy; if you get a bad one, you will become a philosopher.

-Socrates

- If everybody minded their own business, the world would go around a great deal faster than it does.

-Lewis Carroll

- There is no abstract art. You must almost start with something real. Afterward you can remove all traces of reality.

  -Pablo Picasso

- Undoubtedly, philosophers are in the right when they tell us that nothing is great or little otherwise than by comparison.

  -Jonathan Swift

- No matter how busy a man is, he is never too busy to stop and talk about how busy he is.

  -Kahlil Gibran

- The trouble with being punctual is that nine times out of ten, there is nobody to appreciate it.

  -Franklin P. Jones

- One reason why I don't drink is because I wish to know when I am having a good time.

  -Nancy Witcher Astor

- There was no "Before" the beginning of our universe, because once upon a time there was no time.

  -John D Barrow

- I will never be an old man. To me, old age is always 15 years older than I am.

  -Francis Bacon

- Books are where things are explained to you; life is where things aren't. Books make sense of life. The only problem is that the lives they make sense of are other people's lives, never your own.

-J.P Barnes

- When a man says – 'Darling, only two minutes left in the game'. It is the same amount of time when his wife says –'I will be ready in two minutes'.

-Anonymous

- There is no way to find out why a snorer can't hear himself snore.

-Mark Twain

- On the plus side, death is one of the few things that can be done just as easily lying down.

-Woody Allen

- The secrets of a happy marriage – when you are wrong, admit it; when you are right keep mum.

-Anonymous

- Patience is something you admire in the driver behind you and scorn in the one ahead.

-Mac Mccleary

- When you are dead, you don't know that you are dead. It is difficult only for the others. It is the same when you are stupid.

–Anonymous

- Fatigue is the best pillow.

-Benjamin Franklin

- Politics is the art of looking for trouble, finding it everywhere, diagnosing it incorrectly and applying the wrong remedies.

-Groucho Marx

- So that means you need to know things even when you don't need to know. You need to know them not because you need to know them but because you need to know whether or not you need to know. And if you don't need to know you still need to know so that you know that there is no need to know.

-Jonathan Lynn

- Any fool can criticise, condemn, and complain and most fools do.

-Dale C Amegie

- The best way to teach your kids about taxes is by eating 30% of their ice-cream.

-Anonymous

- The time you enjoy wasting is not wasted time.

-Bertrand Russell

- Laughter is a tonic – physical, mental, spiritual. It is a dry cleaner that cleanses you from the inside. It gives a new tone to your life. The day on which you have not laughed is a lost day, indeed:

-Dada JP Vaswani

- Most novices picture themselves as masters and are content with the picture.

-Jean Toomer

- Men who have a pierced ear are better prepared for marriage – they've experienced pain and bought jewellery.

-Rita Rudner

· The time to relax is when you don't have time for it.

-Sydney Harris

· Nothing is permanent in this wicked world--not even our problems.

–Charlie Chaplin

৪৩

~~~~~~

"*HAIR*
Babies haven't any hair;
Old men's heads are just as bare-
Between the cradle and the grave
Lies a haircut and a shave"

-Samuel Wolfenstein

~~~~~~

৪৩

XV
New Horizons

⅋

"SOLITUDE

Laugh, and the world laughs with you;
Weep and you weep alone;
For the sad old earth must borrow its mirth,
But has trouble enough of its own.

Sing, and the hills will answer;
Sigh, it is lost on the air;
The echoes bound to a joyful sound,
But shrink from voicing care.

Rejoice, and men will seek you;
Grieve, and they turn and go;
They want full measure of all your pleasure,
But they do not need your woe.

Be glad, and your friends are many;
Be sad, and you lose them all;
There are none to decline your nectared wine,
But alone you must drink life's gall.

Feast, and your halls are crowded;
Fast, and the world goes by;
Succeed and give, and it helps you live,
But no man can help you die.

There is room in the halls of pleasure
For a large and lordly train,
But one by one we must all file on
Through the narrow aisles of pain. "

-Ella Wheeler Wilcox

OPENING QUOTE

ॐ

~~~~~~

"Every person needs to take one day away. A day in which one consciously separates the past from the future. Jobs, family, employers, and friends can exist one day without any one of us, and if our egos permit us to confess, they could exist eternally in our absence. Each person deserves a day away in which no problems are confronted, no solutions searched for. Each of us needs to withdraw from the cares which will not withdraw from us."

-Maya Angelou

~~~~~~

ॐ

NEW HORIZONS

- When leading, be generous with the community, honourable in action, sincere in your words, as for the rest, do not be concerned.

  -Gautam Buddha

- Be silent and safe. Silence never betrays you.

  –John Boyle O'Reilly

- Art reflects confidence, vigour and optimism by using symbols of progress, speed and power.

  -Anonymous

- There is no end to education. It is not that you read a book, pass an examination and finish with education. The whole of life, from the moment you are born to the moment you die, is a process of learning.

  -J.Krishnamurti

- We give the name of scientist to the type of man who has felt experiment to be a means guiding him its fascinating secrets, and who, in this pursuit, has felt arising within him a love for the mysteries of nature, so passionate as to annihilate the thought of himself.

  -Maria Montessori

- Humility is the strength of the strong and the instrument the wise use to reform their foes.

  -Chanakya

- I hold flesh food to be unsuited to our species. We err in copying the lower animal world, if we are superior to it.

-Joseph Addison

- With the feeling of being special, ambition enters, comparison enters, jealousy enters, conflict enters. Then you start pulling others down.

-George Bush

- A friend is a person who knows all about you and still likes you anyway.

-Elbert Hubbard

- Of all the things you wear, your expression is the most important.

-Janet Lane

- Get busy, keep busy, it is the cheapest kind of medicine there is on earth.

-Dale Carnegie

- The causes of event are always more important than the event itself.

-Marcus Tullis Cicero

- The art of hospitality is to make guest feel at home when you wish they were not.

-Donald Coggan

- No mind is thoroughly well organized that is deficient in a sense of humour.

-Samuel Taylor Coleridge

- Our senses don't deceive us, our judgement does.

-Johann Wolfgang Von Goethe

- For the most of mankind, gratitude is merely a secret desire of further favours.

-Francois de La Rochefoucauld

- Fun has a sacred dimension.

-Adriana Diaz

- Happiness is not found at the end of the road; it is experienced along the way.

–Dearry

- Good manners and good morals are sworn friends and fast allies.

-C.A. Bartol

- The ultimate measure of a man is not where he stands in moments of comfort and convenience, but where he stands at time of challenge and controversy.

-Martin Luther King Jr

- I think our horizon is so vast and Indian culture is so rich that today, culturally, we have a unique position and I don't think one lifetime is enough to encompass it.

-M.F. Husain

- Education is the ability to listen to almost anything without losing your temper or your self-confidence.

-Robert Frost

- Laughter is the shortest distance between two people.

-Victor Borge

- In life there are no problems; there are the solutions waiting to be found.

–Proverb

- Happy marriages begin when we marry the ones we love, and they blossom when we love the ones we marry.

-Tom Muller

- Suffering is a passage, not a dead end.

–Anonymous

- A good answer is one that knows when to stop.

-Anonymous

- Most successful people are just common people who apply themselves in an uncommon way.

-Anonymous

- A quitter never wins and a winner never quits.

-Vince Lombardi

- Beauty is truly just a skin deep, character and performance only last.

–Proverb

- More a child feels valued, the better their values will be.

–Anonymous

- Rudeness is a weak man's imitation of strength.-Eric Hoffer
- He who goes out of his house in search of happiness runs after a shadow.

-Chinese Proverb

- A mind that is stretched by a new experience can never be back to its old dimensions.

-Oliver Wendell Holmes Jr

- A speech is a solemn responsibility. The man who makes a bad thirty minute speech to two hundred people wastes only a half-hour of his own time, but he wastes one hundred hours of the audience's time; more than four days.

-Jenkin Lloyd Jones

- Many individuals have, like uncut diamonds, shining qualities beneath a rough exterior.

–Juvenal

- Ideas are a capital that bears interest only in the hands of talent.

-Antoine De Rivarol

- Obedience alone gives the right to command.

-Ralph Waldo Emerson

- Well arranged time is the surest mark of a well arranged mind.

-Oliver Wendell Holmes Jr

- Only two things are infinite--the universe and human stupidity, and I am not sure about the former.

-Albert Einstein

ॐ

~~~~~~

"ANGER
I was angry with my friend,
I told my wrath, my wrath did end.
I was angry with my foe,
I told it not, my wrath did grow."

-William Blake

~~~~~~

ॐ

XVI
Online

"Let someone call me good or bad,
Let riches come or turn away,
Whether I live for million years,
Or I face death this very day,

Whether someone does frighten me,
Or even tempt me in some way,
May my steps never falter,
From a proven good and righteous way."

-Anonymous

OPENING QUOTE

ॐ

~~~~~~

"Science and religion are two windows that people look through, trying to understand the big universe outside, and why we are here. The two windows give different views (neither is complete), but they look out at the same universe. Both leave out essential features of the real world. And both are worthy of respect."

-Freeman Dyson

~~~~~~

ॐ

ONLINE

- A smile is a curve that can set everything straight.

-Phyllis Diller

- Wealth is a dangerous inheritance, unless the inheritor is trained to active benevolence.

-Anonymous

- Intellectuals solve problems, geniuses prevent them.

-Albert Einstein

- I have learned to seek my happiness by limiting my desires, rather than in attempting to satisfy them.

-John Stuart Mill

- The greatest mistakes we make in our relationship- we listen half, understand quarter, think zero and react double.

-Anonymous

- Every morning you have two choices- continue to sleep with dreams or wake up and chase your dreams.

-Anonymous

- Three nice thoughts: "Kill tension before tension kills you" , "Reach your goal before goal kicks you" , "Live life before life leaves you".

-Anonymous

- A pessimist is somebody who complains about noise when opportunity knocks.

-Anonymous

- Too often we...... enjoy the comfort of opinion without the discomfort of thought.

-John F. Kennedy

- If it does not open, it's not your door.

-Anonymous

- People inspire you, or they drain you, pick them wisely.

-Hans F Hasen

- Don't find fault, find a remedy.

-Henry Ford

- No act of kindness, no matter how small, is ever wasted.

-Anonymous

- Look back, and smile on perils past.

-Walter Scott

- Accountability breeds responsibility.

-Stephen Covey

- Persist while others are quitting.

-William A Ward

- The best thing about a picture is that it never changes, even when the people in it do

-Soumitra Das

- Nothing is more difficult, therefore more precious, than to be able to decide.

-Napoleon Bonaparte

- Education is an admirable thing, but it is well to remember from time to time that nothing that is worth knowing can be taught.

-Oscar Wilde

- In individuals, insanity is rare; but in groups, parties, nations and epochs, it is the rule.

-Anonymous.

- When in doubt, tell the truth. It will confound your enemies and astound your friends

-Mark Twain

- Be not simply good – be good for something.

-Henry David Thoreau

- The greatest tragedy of science: the slaying of a beautiful hypothesis by an ugly fact.

-Thomas Huxley

- Be great in act, as you have been in thought.

-Jean Paul

- The reason that worry kills more people than work is because there are more people who worry than work.

–Anonymous

- If animals could talk, would we then dare to kill and eat them? How could we then justify such fratricide?

-Voltaire

- To be is to do.

--Immanuel Kant

- If animals could talk, would we then dare to kill and eat them? How could we then justify such fratricide?

-Voltaire

- A book is like a garden carried in a pocket.

–Anonymous

- If you have an apple and I have an apple and we exchange these apples then you and I will still each have one apple. But if you have an idea and I have an idea and we exchange these ideas, then each of us will have two ideas.

–George Bernard Shaw

- A house is made with walls and beams; a home is built with love and dream.

-Ralph Waldo Emerson

- A leader is one who knows the way, goes the way, and shows the way.

-John Maxwell

ଈୠ

~~~~~~

"Here none to perfect bliss attain;
The soul in pleasure suffering lies;
Joy hath an undertone of pain,
And even the happiest hours their sighs."

-Henry Wadsworth Longfellow

~~~~~~

ଈୠ

XVII

Pearls

ಐ

If you can keep your head when all about you
Are losing theirs and blaming it on you,
If you can trust yourself when all men doubt you,
But make allowance for their doubting too;

.

If you can wait and not be tired by waiting,
Or being lied about, don't deal in lies
Or being hated, don't give way to hating,
And yet don't look too good, nor talk too wise:

.

If you can dream – and not make dreams your master;
If you can think – and not make thoughts your aim;
If you can meet with triumph and disaster
And treat those two impostors just the same;

.

If you can bear to hear the truth you've spoken
Twisted by knaves to make a trap for fools,
Or watch the things you gave your life to, broken,
And stoop and build 'em up with worn-out tools:

.

If you can make one heap of all your winnings

And risk it on one turn of pitch- and – toss,
And lose, and start again at your beginnings
And never breathe a word about your loss;

If you can force your heart and nerve and sinew
To serve your turn long after they are gone,
And so hold on when there is nothing in you
Except the will which says to them: 'Hold on!'

If you can talk with crowds and keep your virtue,
Or walk with kings – nor lose the common touch,
If neither foes nor loving friends can hurt you,
If all men count with you, but none too much;

If you can fill the unforgiving minute
With sixty seconds' worth of distance run-
Yours is the Earth and everything that's in it,
And – which is more – you'll be a man, my son!"

-Rudyard Kipling

OPENING QUOTE

ॐ

~~~~~~

"*From now on to the end of my life, I will observe equality towards all creatures. I will not do anything sinful either with my mind or speech or body, nor will I get it done by anybody, nor approve of any such thing done by others. I repent for all the sins I have committed until now and desist from them.*"

-Lord Mahavira

~~~~~~

ॐ

PEARLS

- God could not be everywhere and therefore he made mothers.

-Rudyard Kipling

- Death is not the greatest loss in life. The greatest loss is what dies inside us while we are alive.

-Norman Cousins

- Every gun that is made, every warship launched, every rocket fired signifies, in the final sense, a theft from those who hunger and are not fed, those who are cold and are not clothed. This world in arms is not spending money alone. It is spending the sweat of its labourers, the genius of its scientists, the hope of its children.

-Dwight David Eisenhower

- I expect to pass through this world but once. Any good thing, therefore, that I can do, or any kindness that I can show to any fellow creature, let me do it now.....for I shall not pass this way again.

-S. Grellet

- The only thing you take with you when you are gone is what you leave behind.

-John Allston

- A bit of fragrance always clings to the hand that gives roses.

-Chinese Proverb

- Our talents are the gift that God gives to us. What we make of our talents is our gift back to God.

-Leo Buscaglia

- True wealth is what you are, not what you have.

–Anonymous

- Sharp daggers only wound the flesh, but a sharp tongue wounds the spirit.

-Lord Chesterfield

- Never deprive someone of hope; it might be all he has.

-H. Jackson Brown Jr

- Be loyal to them who are not present. In doing so, you win the trust of those who are present.

-Stephen Covey

- Service is the rent we pay for the privilege of living on this earth.

-Shirley Chisholm

- Hospitality must be extended even towards an enemy who comes to your house; the tree does not withdraw its shade from the wood-cutter.

-Indian proverb

- God! Grant me the serenity to accept the things I cannot change, the courage to change things I can, and the wisdom to know the difference.

-Reinhold Neibuhr

- The hands that help are holier than the lips that pray.

-Robert G. Ingersoll

- Always forgive your enemies, nothing annoys them so much.

-Oscar Wilde

- What lies behind us and what lies before us are tiny matters compared to what lies within us.

-Oliver Wendell Holmes

- Being willing to change allows you to move from a point of view to a viewing point – a higher, more expansive place, from which you can see both sides.

-Thomas Crum

- Time goes, you say? Ah, no ! Alas, time stays, we go.

-Austin Dobson

- The greatest use of life is to spend it for something that will outlast it.

-Acharya Tulsi

- He knew how to be poor without the least hint of squalor or inelegance..........he chose to be rich by making his wants few.

-Ralph Waldo Emerson

- The well of providence is deep. It's the buckets we bring to it that are small.

-Mary Webb

- The bee is more honoured than other animals, not because she labours but she labours for others.

-John Chrysostom

- They are never alone that are accompanied with noble thoughts.

  -Sir Philip Sidney

- Man is not the only claimant to all the resources of this earth.

  -R.Krishnaswamy

- The world is my country, all mankind are my brethren, and to do good is my religion.

  -Thomas Paine

- It's easy to bring a smile on someone's lips, but you've truly succeeded if you bring a twinkle in his eyes.

  -Anonymous

- If you and I are having a single thought of violence or hatred against anyone in the world at this moment, we are contributing to the wounding of the world.

  -Deepak Chopra

- Thou shouldst not have been old till thou hadst not been wise.

  –Shakespeare

- It is not "forgive and forget" as if nothing wrong had even happened, but "forgive and go forward" building on the mistakes of the past and the energy generated by reconciliation to create a new future.

  -Anonymous

ജ

~~~~~~

"*I sent my soul through the invisible,*
Some letter of that after-life to spell,
And by and by my soul returned to me,
And answered 'myself am heaven and hell'."

-Omar Khayyam

~~~~~~

ജ

XVIII
Persistence

*"**IT COULDN'T BE DONE***

.

Somebody said that it couldn't be done,
But he with a chuckle replied-
That "may be it couldn't" but he would be one
Who wouldn't say so till he'd tried.

.

So he buckled right in with the trace of a grin
On his face. If he worried, he hid it.
He started to sing as he tackled the thing
That couldn't be done, and he did it."

-Edgar Guest

OPENING QUOTE

~~~~~~

"Nothing in the world can take the place of persistence. Talent will not: nothing is more common than unsuccessful men with talent. Genius will not: unrewarded genius is almost a proverb. Education will not: the world is full of educated derelicts."

-Calvin Coolidge

~~~~~~

PERSISTENCE

- As long as you live, keep learning how to live.

-Lucius Annaeus Seneca

- A man has three names: the name he inherited, the name his parents gave him and the name he makes for himself. I would rather make my name than inherit it.

-William Makepeace Thackeray

- Even if it's absurd to think you can change things, it's even more absurd to think that it's foolish and unimportant to try.

-Peter Charles Newman

- Success doesn't come to you, you have to go to it.

-Marva Collins

- I am always busy which is perhaps the chief reason why I am always well.

-Elizabeth Stanton

- No one has ever drowned in sweat.

-Lou Holtz

- Just as iron rusts from disuse, even so does inaction spoil the intellect.

-Leonardo da Vinci

- Luck is what you have left over after you give 100 percent.

-Langston Coleman

- The successful person makes a habit of doing what the failing person doesn't like to do.

-Thomas Alva Edison

- I am a great believer in luck, and I find the harder I work, the luckier I get.

–Thomas Jefferson

- An ounce of action is worth a ton of theory.

-Frederick Ingels

- The secret of getting things done is to act!

-Dante Alighieri

- Destiny is not a matter of choice; it is not a thing to be waited for, it is a thing to be achieved.

-William Jennings Bryan

- Perspiration, persistence and patience make an unbeatable combination for success.

-Napolean Hill

- If you can't fly then run, if you can't run then walk, if you can't walk then crawl. You have to keep moving.

-Martin Luther King Jr

- The saddest people I've ever met in life are the ones who don't care deeply about anything at all. Passion and satisfaction go hand in hand, and without them, any happiness is only temporary, because there's nothing to make it last.

-Nicholas Sparks

- Know the true value of time; snatch, seize, and enjoy every moment of it. No idleness, no laziness, no procrastination; never put off till tomorrow what you can do today.

-Lord Chesterfield

- There are but two ways of rising in the world: either by one's own industry or profiting by the foolishness of others.

-La Bruyere

- I have ever held it as a maxim never to do that through another which it was possible for me to execute myself.

–Montesquieu

- I have nothing to offer but blood, toil, tears and sweat.

-Winston Churchill

- Be not afraid of growing slowly; be afraid only of standing still.

-Chinese Proverb

- Genius is one percent inspiration and ninety-nine percent perspiration.

-Thomas Alva Edison

- Never discourage anyone who continually makes progress, no matter how slow.

-Plato

- All the birds find shelter during rain, but the eagle avoids rain by flying above the clouds. Problems are common but attitude makes the difference.

-Dr A.P.J Abdul Kalam

- Earn a reputation for achieving by meeting deadlines and getting things done.

–Anonymous

- Perfect freedom is reserved for the man who lives by his own work and, in that work, does achieve what he wants to do.

-Robin G. Collingwood

- When life changes to be harder, change yourself to be stronger.

-Anonymous

- Teachers open the doors, but you must enter by yourself.

-Mother Teresa

- Good, better, best, never let it rest, till your good is better & your better is best.

-St. Jerome

ಞ

~~~~~~

"Good, Better, Best.
Never let it rest.
Till your good is better
And your better is best."

-St. Jerome

~~~~~~

ಞ

XIX
Politics

&

"*TO INDIA*

O young through all thy immemorial years!
Rise, Mother, rise, regenerated from thy gloom,
And, like a bride high-mated with the spheres,
Beget new glories from thine ageless womb!

The nations that in fettered darkness weep
Crave thee to lead them where great mornings break...
Mother, O Mother, wherefore dost thou sleep?
Arise and answer for thy children's sake!

Thy future calls thee with a manifold sound
To crescent honours, splendours, victories vast;
Waken, O slumbering Mother and be crowned,
Who once wert empress of the sovereign past."

-Sarojini Naidu

&

OPENING QUOTE

ॐ

~~~~~~

"I have travelled the length and breadth of India. I have not seen one person who is a beggar, who is a thief. Such wealth I have seen in this country, such high moral values, people of such nature that I do not think we would ever conquer this country, unless we break the very backbone of this nation which is her spiritual and cultural heritage. And therefore I propose that we replace her old and ancient education system, her culture. For if Indians think that all that is foreign and English is good and greater than their own, they will become what we want them –black English people –a truly dominated slave nation."

-Macaulay's letter to British Government, 2nd Feb, 1835

~~~~~~

ॐ

<u>Special note of ponderance</u>-

While we, as Indians, shall curse Macaulay for destroying the values embodied in the culture and character of our country, we may also feel inclined to admit that he by his sheer strategy and calculation served his country no less than its soldiers and scientists. If a single man's foresight could reduce us to a "truly dominated slave nation", can't we, as a whole nation, reverse that damage and, through our collective efforts, regain our past glory fast?

-from the compiler of this book

ॐ

POLITICS

- 'Poli' is a latin word meaning 'many' and 'tics' meaning 'blood sucking creatures'.

-Robin Williams

- There may be a time when we are powerless to prevent injustice, but there must never be a time when we fail to protest.

-Elie Wiesel

- If you can't convince them, confuse them.

-Harry S. Truman

- Who makes up the majority in any given country? Is it the wise men or the fools? I think we must agree that the fools are in a terrible overwhelming majority all the wide world over.

-Henrik Ibsen

- I offer my opponents a bargain; if they will stop telling lies about us, I will stop telling the truth about them.

-Robert Louis Stevenson

- It is the duty of the government to make it difficult for people to do wrong; easy to do right.

-William Ewart Gladstone

- Those who make peaceful revolution impossible will make violent revolution inevitable.

-John F. Kennedy

- Diplomacy is more than saying or doing right things at the right time, it's avoiding saying or doing wrong things at any time.

-Bo Bennett

- Nothing could be more dangerous to the existence of a republic than to introduce religion into politics.

-Robert Green Ingersoll

- Patriotism is, fundamentally, a conviction that a particular country is the best in the world because you were born in it.

-George Bernard Shaw

- Politics is war without bloodshed.

-Mao Zedong

- The primary factor in a successful attack is speed.

-Louis Mountbatten

- Purpose of foreign policy is not to provide an outlet for our own sentiments; it's to shape real events in a real world.

-John F. Kennedy

- A moment comes, which comes but rarely in history, when we step out from the old to the new, when an age ends, and when the soul of a nation, long suppressed, finds utterance.

-Jawaharlal Nehru

- Peace is not merely a distant goal that we seek, but a means by which we arrive at that goal.

-Martin Luther King Jr

- I confess that I cannot understand how we can plot, lie, cheat and commit murder abroad and remain humane, honourable, trustworthy and trusted at home.

-Archibald Cox

- When leaders act contrary to the conscience of the constitution, we must act contrary to leaders.

-Jaiprakash Narayan

- The politician is trained in the art of inexactitude. His words tend to be blunt or rounded, because if they have a cutting edge they may later return to wound him.

-Edward Murrow

- Lawless are those that make their wills their law.

-William Shakespeare

- Politicians are the same all over. They promise to build a bridge even when there is no river.

-Nikita Khrushchev

- Judges must beware of hard constructions and strained inferences; for there is no worse torture than the torture of laws.

-Francis Bacon

- Only the government can take perfectly good paper, cover it with perfectly good ink and make the combination worthless.

-Milton Friedman

- You do not lead by hitting people over the head —that's assault, not leadership.

-Dwight D. Eisenhower

- In Mexico an air conditioner is called a politician because it makes a lot of noise but doesn't work very well.

-Len Deighton

- The test of courage comes when we are in the minority. The test of tolerance comes when we are in the majority.

-Ralph Washington Sockman

- Charity begins at home. Likewise, obedience to law too should first come from the rulers and the administrators.

-Chanakya

- Opposition unites. From what draws apart results the most beautiful harmony. All things take place by strife.

-Heraclitus

- Leadership needs to shift from perpetuating the status quo to being a catalyst of change.

-Geetanjali Kirloskar

- Justice and power must be brought together, so that whatever is just may be powerful, and whatever is powerful may be just.

-Blaise Pascal

- This world needs leaders who take a little greater share of the blame and a little smaller share of the credit.

-John C. Maxwell

- Hope nothing from foreign governments. They will never be really willing to aid you until you have shown that you are strong enough to conquer without them.

-Giuseppe Mazzini

- The deterioration of a government begins almost always by the decay of its principles.

-Montesquieu

- To know the pains of power, we must go to those who have it, to know its pleasure, we must go to those who have it, to know its pleasures, we must go to those who are seeking it. The pains of power are real, its pleasure imaginary.

-Charles Caleb Colton

- Mr. Prime Minister, since your government is more corrupt than ever before, we have to be more impatient than ever before.

-Sushma Swaraj

- Secrecy, being an instrument of conspiracy, ought never to be a system of regular government.

-Jawaharlal Nehru

- The end of law is not to abolish or restrain, but to preserve and enlarge freedom... where there is no law, there is no freedom.

-John Locke

- Compromise makes a good umbrella, but a poor roof; it is temporary expedient, often wise in party politics, almost sure to be unwise in statesmanship.

-James Russell Lowell

- Written laws are like spiders' webs, and will, like them, only entangle and hold the poor and weak, while the rich and powerful will easily break through them.

–Anacharsis

- A leader is a dealer in hope.

-Napoleon Bonaparte

- Polity is the art of looking for trouble, finding it everywhere, diagnosing it incorrectly and applying the wrong remedies.

-Groucho Marx

- A politician thinks of the next election; a statesman of the next generation.

-James Freeman Clarke

- The art of taxation consists in so plucking the goose as to obtain the largest amount of feathers with the least possible amount of hissing.

-J.B Colbert

- Justice will not be served until those who are unaffected are as outraged as those who are.

-Benjamin Franklin

- Government is a trust, and the officers of the government are trustees; and both the trust and the trustees are created for the benefit of the people.

-Henry Clay

- A return to first principles in a republic is sometimes caused by the simple virtues of one man. His good example has such an influence that the good men strive to imitate him, and the wicked are ashamed to lead a life so contrary to his example.

-Niccolo Machiavelli

- There is no crueller tyranny than that which is perpetuated under the shield of law and in the name of justice.

-Charles De Montesquieu

- Any change is resisted because bureaucrats have a vested interest in the chaos in which they exist.

-Richard M Nixon

- A true leader will neither complain nor explain, and is open to learning all the time. Admitting a past mistake and creating space for others with completely diverse viewpoints can make a leader more acceptable, universal. A leader does not pass the buck.

-Sri Sri Ravi Shankar

- When you can't make them see the light, make them feel the heat.

-Ronald Reagan

- There will be no end to the troubles of states, or of humanity itself. Till philosophers become kings and rulers become philosophers, and political power and philosophy thus come into the same hands.

-Plato

- You call my candidate a horse thief, and I call yours lunatic, and we both know it's just till election day.

-Stephen Vincent Benet

- The true soldier fights not because he hates what is in front of him, but because he loves what is behind him.

-G.K. Chesterton

- Politics is the last refuge of a scoundrel.

-Dr Samuel Johnson

- The test of courage comes when we are in the minority. The test of tolerance comes when we are in the majority.

-Ralph W Sockman

ॐ

"When after many battles past,
Both tir'd with blows, make peace at last.
What is it, after all, the people get?
Why: taxes, windows, wooden legs, and debt."

-Frances Moore

ॐ

XX
Rainbow

“YOUR DREAMS
Hold on to your dreams,
And don't let go!

.

Follow the rainbow,
The tide in its flow,

.

Salute the sun at the break of the day
Find time for the flowers along the way

.

Follow the birds as they come and go.
Hold on to your dreams, And don't let go!”

-Ruskin Bond

OPENING QUOTE

恓

~~~~~~

"*Next to being right in this world, the best of all things is to be clearly and definitely wrong. If you go buzzing about between right and wrong, vibrating and fluctuating, you come out nowhere; but if you are absolutely and thoroughly and persistently wrong you must, some of these days, have the extreme good fortune of knocking your head against the fact, and that sets you all straight again.*"

-Thomas Henry Huxley

~~~~~~

恓

RAINBOW

- Who in the rainbow can draw the line where the violet tint ends and the orange tint begins? Distinctly we see the difference of the colours, but where exactly does the one first blindingly enter into the other? So with sanity and insanity.

-Herman Melville

- The mark of the immature man is that he wants to die nobly for a cause, while the mark of a mature man is that he wants to live humbly for one.

-J.D Salinger

- What we have done for ourselves alone dies with us; what we have done for others, remains and is immortal.

-Albert Pike

- Courage is what it takes to stand up and speak; courage is also what it takes to sit down and listen.

-Winston Churchill

- In the sky, there is no distinction between east and west; people create distinctions out of their own minds and then believe them to be true.

-Gautam Buddha

- I don't like work - no man does, but I like what is in the work - the chance to find yourself.

-Joseph Conrad

- No matter how fast you run, your shadow more than keeps up, sometimes it's in front.

–Rumi

- As often as the mind is outgoing, so often it should be turned within.

-Sri Ramana Maharshi

- Success is to be measured not so much by the position that one has reached in life as by the obstacles which he has overcome.

-Booker T. Washington

- It is thousand times better to have common sense without education than to have education without common sense.

-Robert Green Ingersoll

- A room without books is like a body without a soul.

-Sir John Lubbock

- Worry is interest paid on trouble before it becomes due.

-Sir William Ralph Inge

- Remember that the person you consider most ignorant and insignificant is the one who came from God, so that he might be able to learn bliss from grief and knowledge from gloom.

-Kahlil Gibran

- Thought is the labour of the intellect, reverie is its pleasure.

-Victor Hugo

- A right exterior conduct really has its secret in a true interior life.

-Andrew Greeley

- Gratitude is the fairest blossom which springs from the soul.

-Henry Ward Beecher

- Everyone wants happiness, no one wants pain, but you can't make a rainbow without a little rain.

-Anonymous

- Animals are such agreeable friends- they ask no questions; they pass no criticisms.

-George Eliot

- Forgiveness is a perfectly selfish act. It sets you free from the past.

-Brian Tracy

- The human race has one really effective weapon, and that is laughter.

-Mark Twain

- If you've had a good time playing the game, you're a winner even if you lose.

-Malcolm Forbes

- If Columbus had turned back, no one would have blamed him. Of course, no one would have remembered him then either.

-Anonymous

- Two things define you –your determination when you have nothing; your attitude when you have everything.

-Anonymous

- It is better to deserve honours and not have them, than to have them and not deserve them.

-Mark Twain

- Science might almost be redefined as the process of substituting unimportant questions which can be answered, for important questions which cannot.

-Kenneth Ewart Boulding

- Remember the main thing is to keep the main thing the main thing.

-Stephen Covey

- Books link and join generations; women save and protect the threads of life from breaking apart.

-Mikhail Gorbachev

- Brevity is the soul of wit.

-William Shakespeare

- The true reason I read is to feel less alone, to make a connection with a consciousness other than my own.

-Zadie Smith

- Peace is of the nature of a conquest; for then both parties nobly are subdued, and neither party loses.

-William Shakespeare

- Concentrate all your thoughts upon the work at hand. The sun's rays do not burn until brought to a focus.

-Alexander Graham Bell

- Words mean more than what is set down on paper. It takes the human voice to infuse them with shades of deeper meaning.

-Maya Angelou

- Education makes people easy to lead, but difficult to drive; easy to govern, but impossible to enslave.

-Lord Brougham

- Nature, time and patience are the three great physicians.

-Henry George Bohn

- I disapprove of what you say, but I will defend to the death your right to say it.

–Voltaire

- Some are weather-wise, some are otherwise.

-Benjamin Franklin

- Right actions are the best apologies for wrong ones in the past.

-Tyron Edwards

- Talent develops itself in solitude; character develops in the stream of lie.

-Johann Wolfgang Von Goethe

- Don't forget that a couple of words of praise or encouragement can make someone's day

-H. Jackson Brown Jr

- A single conversation across the table with a wise man is better than ten years of study of books.

-Henry Wadsworth Longfellow

- No one is too poor to help another and no one is too rich to never need help.

-Anonymous

- Life always offers you a SECOND CHANCE. It's called TOMORROW.

-Nicholas Sparks

- He who angers you conquers you.

-Elizabeth Kenny

- Live as if you were to die tomorrow. Learn as if you were to live forever.

-M.K Gandhi

- Try to be a rainbow in someone's cloud.

-Maya Angelou

૪૭

~~~~~~

"No work so great, but what admits decay,
No act so glorious, but must fade away-
Old things must yield to new, common to strange,
Perpetual motion, brings perpetual change."

-James Miller

~~~~~~

૪૭

XXI
Spring Time

"LAUGH AND BE MERRY

Laugh and be merry, remember, better the world with a song,
Better the world with a blow in the teeth of a wrong.
Laugh, for the time is brief, a thread the length of a span,
Laugh and be proud to belong to the old proud pageant of man.

Laugh and be merry, remember, in olden time
God made heaven and earth for joy, he took in a rhyme,
Made them, and filled them full with the strong red wine of his
mirth
The splendid joy of the stars: the joy of the earth.

So we must laugh and drink from the deep blue cup of the sky,
Join the jubilant song of the great stars sweeping by.
Laugh, and battle, and work, and drink of the wine outpoured
In the dear green earth, the sign of the joy of the Lord.

Laugh and be merry together, like brothers akin,
Guesting awhile in the rooms of a beautiful inn.
Glad till the dancing stops, and the lilt of the music ends,
Laugh till the game is played, and be you merry, my friends."

-John Masefield

OPENING QUOTE

ॐ

~~~~~~

"If there is one place on the face of earth where all the dreams of living men have found a home from the very earliest days when man began the dreams of existence, it is India."

-Romain Rolland

~~~~~~

ॐ

SPRING TIME

- I refuse to accept that mankind is so tragically bound to the starless midnight of racism and war that the bright daybreak of peace and brotherhood can never become a reality.

   -Martin Luther King Jr

- A little house well filled, a little land well tilled and a little wife well willed, are great riches.

   -Proverb

- We are all serving a life sentence and good behaviour is our only hope for a pardon.

   -Douglas Horton

- There is frequently more to be learned from the unexpected questions of a child than the discourses of men.

   -John Locke

- Slow down and enjoy life. It's not only the scenery you miss by going too fast; you also miss the sense of where you are going and why.

   -Eddie Cantor

- A smile costs nothing but creates much – it lights the face, warms the heart.

   -Anonymous

- A speech is a poetry, cadence, rhythm, imagery, sweep...... and reminds us that words, like children, have the power to make dance the dullest bean-bag of a heart.

-Peggy Noonan

- Peace is not a relationship between nations. It is a condition of mind brought about by a serenity of the soul.

-Jawaharlal Nehru

- Someone will always be looking at you as an example of how to behave. Don't let them down.

-H. Jackson Brown Jr

- A man travels the world over in search of what he needs and returns home to find it.

-George Moore

- Cherish all happy moments; they make fine cushion for old age.

-Christopher Morley

- Everything we humans make or manufacture, we eventually tire of, what is made or created by nature, never wearies us.

-Peter Mortimer

- Writing is its own reward.

-Henry Miller

- I have not failed. I've just found 10,000 ways that won't work.

-T.A. Edison

- 'Sweet are the sounds of the flute and the lute', say those who have not heard the prattle of their own children.

-St. Thiruvalluvar

- To get things done, choose a busy person. The other kind has no time.

–Anonymous

- You only live once. But if you live right, once is enough.

-Mae West

- The purpose of life is a life of purpose.

-Robert Byrne

- Live a good honourable life. Then when you get older and think back, you'll get to enjoy it a second time.

-Dalai Lama

- The art of being wise is the art of knowing what to overlook.

-William James

- If you are right, there is no need to lose your temper; if you are wrong you have no right to lose your temper.

–Anonymous

- The difference between ordinary and extraordinary is that little extra.

-Jimmy Johnson

- A good book is the best friend, the same today and forever.

-Martin Tupper

- Never chase a lie. Let it alone and it will run itself to death.

-Lyman Beecher

· A single rose can be my garden; a single friend is my world.

-Leo Buscaglia

· The most wasted day of all is that on which we have not laughed.

-Sebastien R.N. Chamfort

· If you know you're going to lose, do it with style.

–Anonymous

· Hope is the power of being cheerful in circumstances which we know to be desperate.

-Gilbert Keith Chesterton

· A good laugh is sunshine in a house.

-William Makepeace Thackery

· Early to bed and early to rise, makes a man healthy, wealthy, and wise.

-Benjamin Franklin

· When you stop trying to change others and work on changing yourself, your world changes for the better.

–Anonymous

· If you have much, give a little of your wealth. If you have little, give a little of your heart.

-Arabic Proverb

· I never lose. I either win or I learn.

-Nelson Mandela

- The bad news is time flies; the good news is you are the pilot.

-Michael Altshuler

- When you really like someone, tell him. Sometimes you only get one chance.

-H. Jackson Brown Jr

- You don't learn to walk away by following rules. You learn by doing and by falling over.

-Richard Branson

- Be not angry that you cannot make others as you wish them to be, since you cannot make yourself as you wish to be.

-Thomas a Kempis

ℚ

"Happy the man, and happy he alone
He who can call today his own
He who, secure within, can say-
"Tomorrow do thy worst, for I have lived today"."

-Horace

ℚ

XXII
Sweet & Sour

ॐ

"SON OF MINE
My son, your troubled eyes search mine,
Puzzled and hurt by colour line.
Your black skin soft as velvet shine;
What can I tell you, son of mine?

.

I could tell you of heartbreak, hatred blind,
I could tell of crime that shame mankind,
Of brutal wrong and deeds malign,
Of rape and murder, son of mine;

.

But I'll tell instead of brave and fine
When lives of black and white entwine,
And men in brotherhood combine –
This would I tell you, son of mine."

-Kathy Walker

ॐ

OPENING QUOTE

ಹಿ

~~~~~~

"When, after a long absence, a man safely returns from afar, his relatives, friends and well-wishers welcome him home on arrival. As kinsmen welcome a dear one on arrival, even so his own good deeds will welcome the doer of good who has gone from this world to the next."

-Dhammapada

~~~~~~

ಹಿ

SWEET AND SOUR

- As soon as I had stepped out of my mother's womb onto dry land, I realized that I had made a mistake...... but the trouble with children is that they are not returnable.

-Quentin Crisp

- Men make counterfeit money; in many more cases, money makes counterfeit men.

-Sydney J. Harris

- It is pretty hard to tell what does bring happiness; poverty and wealth have both failed.

-Kin Hubbard

- It takes in reality only one to make a quarrel. It is useless for the sheep to pass a resolution in favour of vegetarianism, while the wolf remains of a different opinion.

-William Ralph Inge

- The difference between stupidity and genius is that genius has its limits.

-Albert Einstein

- When it comes to privacy and accountability, people always demand the former for themselves and the latter for everyone else.

-David Brin

- I will not let anyone walk through my mind with their dirty feet.

-M.K. Gandhi

- If we can really understand the problem, the answer will come out of it, because the answer is not separate from the problem.

-J. Krishnamurti

- There is no odour so bad as that which arises from goodness tainted.

-Henry David Thoreau

- A long dispute means that both parties are wrong.

–Voltaire

- The more you speak of yourself, the more you are likely to lie.

-Johann Wolfgang Von Goethe

- A thankless man rarely does a thankful deed.

–Proverb

- When money speaks, the truth is silent.

-Russian Proverb

- He who is of the opinion that money can do everything may well be suspected of doing everything for money.

-Benjamin Franklin

- Have you noticed that a narrow mind and a wide mouth often go together?

-Francois de La Rochefoucauld

- No man is rich enough to buy back his past.

-Oscar Wilde

- The only way to get rid of responsibility is to discharge them.

-Walter Robertson

- Nature knows best; she hasn't arranged your anatomy so as to make it easy for you to pat yourself on the back.

-Francois de La Rochefoucauld

- Trust and confidence, like souls, never return once they have departed.

-PubliliusSyrus

- Where all think alike, no one thinks very much.

-Walter Lippmann

- In prosperity our friends know us; in adversity we know our friends.

-John Churton Collins

- Meetings are indispensable when you don't want to do anything.

-J.K. Galbraith

- I am patient with stupidity but not with those who are proud of it.

-Edith Sitwell

- My stomach is not a graveyard for dead animals.

-George Bernard Shaw

- If you really want to do something, you will find a way. If you don't you will find an excuse.

-Jim Rohn

- The only man who never makes a mistake is the person who never does anything.

-Theodore Roosevelt

- If two men agree on everything, you can be sure that one of them is doing all the thinking.

-Lyndon Baines Johnson

- Behind every successful man there's a lot of unsuccessful years.

-Bob Brown

- Ability will never catch up with the demand for it.

-Malcoln Forbes

- Nowadays people know the price of everything and the value of nothing.

-Oscar Wilde

- We can easily forgive a child who is afraid of the dark. The real tragedy of life is when men are afraid of the light.

–Plato

- I don't know who my grandfather was; I am much more concerned to know what his grandson will be.

-Abraham Lincoln

- The greatest of faults, I should say, is to be conscious of none.

-Thomas Carlyle

- Everyone is as God made him, and often a great deal worse.

–Cervantes

- The greatest happiness of life is the conviction that we are loved - loved for ourselves, or rather, loved in spite of ourselves.

-Victor Hugo

- God loved the birds and invented trees. Man loved the birds and invented cages.

-Jacques Deval

- A person will sometimes devote all his life to the development of one part of his body - the wishbone.

-Robert Frost

- Wise men learn more from fools than fools from the wise.

-Cato the Censor

- If you think education is expensive, try ignorance.

-Derek Bok

- Some people are so poor, all they have is money.

–Anonymous

- Speak only when you feel that your words are better than your silence.

–Dr Nosiri

- Inconsistency is the only thing in which men are consistent.

-Horace Smith

- It is easier to know mankind in general than man individually.

-Francois de La Rochefoucauld

- Men make laws; women make manners.

-Joseph Alexandre Pierre De Segur

- Those who never retract their opinions love themselves more than they love truth.

-Joseph Joubert

- You can fool some of the people all of the time, and all of the people some of the time, but you cannot fool all of the people all the time.

-Abraham Lincoln

- The rule of my life is to make business a pleasure, and pleasure my business.

-Aaron Burr

- If men are so wicked with religion, what would they be without it?

-Benjamin Franklin

- The only way to stop smoking is to just stop- no 'ifs' , or 'buts'.

-Edith Zittler

- The accomplice to the crime of corruption is frequently our own indifference.

-Bess Myerson

- People sometimes say the way things happen in the movies is unreal, but actually, it's the way things happen to you in life that's unreal.

-Andy Warhol

- Imagination was given to man to compensate him for what he is not; a sense of humour to console him for what he is.

-Francis Bacon

- Every man is guilty of all the good he did not do.

–Voltaire

- Men are not prisoners of fate, but only prisoners of their own minds.

-Franklin Roosevelt

- It's Christmas Eve! It's the one night of the year when we all act a little nicer, we smile a little easier, and we cheer a little more. For a couple of hours out of the whole year, we are the people that we always hoped we would be.

-Bill Murray

- The origin of all conflict between me and my fellow men is that I don't say what I mean and I don't do what I say.

-Martin Buber

- The mark of higher education isn't the knowledge you accumulate in your head. It's the skills you gain about how to learn.

-Adam Grant

- Only two kinds of people can attain self-knowledge; whose minds are not crowded with thoughts borrowed from others; and those who, after studying all scriptures and science, have come to realise that they know nothing.

-Ramakrishna Paramhansa

- Ignorance is a voluntary misfortune.

-Nicholas Ling

- Sometimes when I consider what tremendous consequences come from little things, I am tempted to think.....there are no little things.

-Bruce Barton

- The problem with the world is that fools and fanatics are always so certain of themselves, but wiser people are so full of doubts.

-Bertrand Russell

- That you may retain your self-respect, it is better to displease the people by doing what you know is right, than to temporarily please them by doing what you know is wrong.

-William J.H. Boetcker

- A life spent making mistakes is not only more honourable, but more useful than a life spent doing nothing.

-George Bernard Shaw

- Life is about learning: when you stop learning, you die.

-Tom Clancy

- If we desire respect for the law, we must first make the law respectable.

-Louis D Brandeis

- The human race has had long experience and a fine tradition in surviving adversity. But we now face a task for which we have little experience, the task of surviving prosperity.

-Alan G Regg

- Avarice is the vice of declining years.

-G. Bancroft

- It is true that those who swim only drown, not the others who remain on the shore but then such people cannot learn swimming either.

-Sardar Vallabh Bhai Patel

- I can easily teach twenty what was good to be done, than be one of the twenty to follow my own teachings.

-Shakespeare

~~~~~~

"LAYS OF ANCIENT ROME
Then out spoke brave Horatius,
The captain of the gate;
"To every man upon this earth
Death cometh soon or late.
And how can man die better
Then facing fearful odds,
For the ashes of his fathers
And the temples of his gods?""

-Lord Macaulay

~~~~~~

XXIII
Thoughts

"IF GOD SHOULD GO ON STRIKE

.

How good it is that
God above has never
Gone on strike
Because he was not
Treated fair in things
He didn't like.

.

If only once he'd
Given up and said,
"That's it, I'm through!
I've had enough of
Those on earth,
So this is what I'll do:

.

I'll give my orders to the sun-
Cut off the heat supply!
And to the moon-
Give no more light,
And to the oceans move dry.

.

Then just to make
Things really tough
And put the pressure on,
Turn off the vital
Oxygen till every
Breath is gone !"

.

You know, He would
Be justified, if
Fairness was the game,
For no one has been
More abused or met
With more disdain.

.

And yet he carries on
Supplying you and me
With all the favour
Of his grace, and
Everything for free.

.

Men say they want a
Better deal, and so
On strike they go,
But what a deal we've
Given God to whom
All things we owe.

.

We don't care whom
We hurt to gain the
Things we like,
But what a mess we'd
All be in, if God
Should go on strike."

-Mary Evelyn Williams

ॐ

OPENING QUOTE

ॐ

~~~~~~

"We do not own the earth. It has only given us a shelter in our journey. We are just transients here and owe it to ourselves to leave this earth a little better than we found it. This is everybody's job; no one is exempt from it and, in this sense, nobody is unemployed."

-Emnath Easwaram

~~~~~~

ॐ

THOUGHTS

- A thought is an idea in transit.

-Pythagoras

- Reverence for life affords me my fundamental principle of morality, namely that good consists in maintaining life, and that to destroy, to harm, or to hinder life is evil.

-Albert Schweitzer

- It is not your aptitude but your attitude that determines your altitude.

-Zig Ziglar

- Half the world does not know how the other half lives.

-Jacob A. Riis

- The purpose of life is not to be happy. It is to be useful, honourable and compassionate, to have it make some difference.

-Ralph Waldo Emerson

- Much unhappiness has come into the world because of bewilderment and things left unsaid.

-Fyodor Dostoyevsky

- We cannot solve problems by using the same kind of thinking we used when we created them.

-Albert Einstein

- True realisation of the actual nature of this material world – its perishable, transitory and illusory aspects- best dawn on a person in suffering.

-Guru Teg Bahadur

- There is little difference in people, but that little difference makes a big difference. The little difference is attitude. The big difference is whether it is positive or negative.

-William Clement Stone

- Science has nothing to be ashamed of, even in the ruins of Nagasaki. The shame is theirs who appeal to other values than the imaginative values which science has evolved.

-Jacob Bronowski

- It's prudent to gain the whole world and lose your own soul. But don't forget that your soul sticks to you if you stick to it; but the world has a way of slipping through your fingers.

-George Bernard Shaw

- There are people in the world so hungry that God cannot appear to them except in the form of bread.

-M.K. Gandhi

- If you take the game of life seriously, if you take your nervous system seriously, if you take your sense organs seriously, if you take the energy process seriously, you must turn on, tune in, and drop out.

-Timothy Francis Leary

- A little while and I will be gone from among you, whither I cannot tell. From nowhere we came, into nowhere we go. What is life? It is a flash of a firefly in the night; it is the breath of a buffalo in the winter time; it is as the little shadow that runs across the grass and loses itself in the sunset.

-Henry Rider Haggard

- Capital punishment is as fundamentally wrong as a cure for crime as charity is wrong as a cure for poverty.

-Henry Ford

- 'An eye for an eye' only leads to more blindness.

-Margaret Atwood

- Discussion is an exchange of intelligence. Argument is an exchange of ignorance.

-Bill Gold

- People who have little and want less are happier than those who have much and still want more.

-Anonymous

- When one door of happiness closes, another opens; but we look so long at the closed door that we do not see one which has opened.

-Helen Keller

- A woman, who creates and sustains a home and under whose hands children grow up to the strong and pure men and women, is a creator second only to god.

-Helen Hunt Jackson

- You cannot reason with a hungry belly; it has no ears.

-Greek Proverb

- It is forbidden to kill; therefore, all murderers are punished unless they kill in large numbers and to the sound of trumpets.

–Voltaire

- Education is an admirable thing, but it is well to remember from time to time that nothing that is worth knowing can be taught.

-Oscar Wilde

- Look into the eyes of the animal you are killing and listen to the voice of your conscience. It loudly prohibits you from taking the life of an innocent and speechless living being.

-Shakahar Kranti

- There are three things that cannot be retrieved: the spoken word, time past and the neglected opportunity.

–Anonymous

- Always look at what you left. Never look at what you have lost.

-Robert H. Schuller

- People who fly into a rage overheat their engines and make bad landings.

-Will Rogers

- Count your blessings and you will lack nothing.

-Dada J.P. Vaswani

- I do not feel obliged to believe that the same God who has endowed us with sense, reason and intellect has intended us to forgo their use.

-Galileo Galilei

- The darkest hour is just before dawn.

–Proverb

- What counts in making a happy marriage is not so much how compatible you are but how you deal with incompatibility.

-Count Leo Tolstoy

- An important thing is to realise one's own insignificance in the scheme of things. Life will go on without missing you very much after you are gone.

–Anonymous

- A good home must be made, not bought.

-Joyce Maynard

- Who is rich? He who is content. Who is that? Nobody.

-Benjamin Franklin

- Anyone can become angry – that is easy. But to be angry with the right person, to the right degree, at the right time, for the right purpose, and in the right way – this is not easy.

–Aristotle

- The animals which we neglect or ill-use are his animals. Cruelty to animals is not only a stupid act of inhumanity to the lower creatures but also an insult to God, whose creatures we are.

-Peter Hoffman

- Consider how much more you often suffer from your anger and grief, than from those very things for which you are angry and grieved.

-Marcus Antonius

- Man - the only animal in the world to fear.

-David Herbert Lawerence

- Death is nothing to us, since when we are, death has not come and when death has come, we are not.

–Epicurus

- Freedom from fear and injustice and oppression will be ours only in the measure that men who value such freedom are ready to sustain its possession - to defend it against every thrust from within or without.

-Dwight David Eisenhower

- A very great part of the mischief that vex this world arises from words.

-Edmund Burke

- Unfaithfulness in the keeping of an appointment is an act of clear dishonesty. You may as well borrow a person's money as his time.

-Horace Mann

- It is curious that physical courage should be so common in the world and moral courage so rare.

-Mark Twain

- Who can cast an evil eye on you if you walk straight with the name of God on your lips. Be convinced at heart that purity itself is a shield.

-M.K. Gandhi

- What has always made a hell on earth has been that man has tried to make it his heaven.

-Friedrich Holderlin

- Until the philosophy which holds one race superior and another inferior is finally and permanently discredited and abandoned, everywhere is war.

-Bob Marley

- An age is called dark, not because light fails to shine, but because people refuse to see it.

-James Michener

- Social justice cannot be attained by violence. Violence kills what it intends to create.

-Pope John Paul II

- Oh! What a tangled web we weave, when we practice to deceive.

-Walter Scott

৪৩

~~~~~~

"TINY LIGHT
Scorn not thy narrow task.
For he who made
The brilliant stars and
Moon to gild the night,
Placed the small glow-worm
In earth's woodland shade,
And bade her too shed
Forth her tiny light."

-Fanny Montgomery

~~~~~~

৪৩

XXIV
Wisdom

"*DO IT ANYWAY*

*People are often
unreasonable, illogical and self-centred;
forgive them anyway.*

*If you are kind, people may accuse
you of selfish, ulterior motives;
be kind anyway.*

*If you are honest and frank,
people may cheat you;
be honest and frank anyway.*

*What you spend years building,
someone could destroy overnight;
build anyway.*

*If you find serenity and happiness
they may be jealous;
be happy anyway.*

The good you do today,
people will often forget tomorrow;
do good anyway.

Give the world the best you have,
and it may never be enough;
give the world the best
you've got anyway. "

-Unkown

ഔ

OPENING QUOTE

ॐ

~~~~~~

"Your time is limited, so don't waste it living someone else's life. Don't be trapped by dogma – which is living with the results of other people's thinking. Don't let the noise of other's opinions drown out your own inner voice. And most important, have the courage to follow your heart and intuition. They somehow already know what you truly want to become. Everything else is secondary."

-Steve Jobs

~~~~~~

ॐ

WISDOM

- To reform a world, to reform a nation no wise men will undertake; and all but foolish men know, that the only solid reformation is what which begins and perfects on himself.

-Thomas Carlyle

- Don't hit at all if it is honourably possible to avoid hitting; but never hit soft.

-Theodore Roosevelt

- Wisdom outweighs any wealth.

–Sophocles

- The golden rule is to test everything in the light of reason and experience, no matter from where it comes.

-M.K. Gandhi

- Don't use words too big for the subject. Don't say 'infinite' when you mean very; otherwise you'll have no word left when you want to talk about something really infinite.

-C.S. Lewis

- Let us not look back in anger, nor forward in fear, but around in awareness.

-James Thurber

- If you must play, decide upon three things at the start: the rules of the game, the stakes, and the quitting time.

-Chinese Proverb

- The best way to keep something bad from happening is to see it ahead of time.

-William Burroughs

- Wisdom and policy dictate that we must do as destiny demands and keep peace with the irresistible march of events.

-Napoleon Bonaparte

- If you ever run into an industry that says it needs better people, sell its shares. There are no better people. You have to use ordinary, every-day people and make them capable of doing the work.

-Peter Ferdinand Drucker

- We gain more by letting ourselves be seen such as we are, then by attempting to appear what we are not.

-Francois de La Rochefoucauld

- The wise man has long ears, big eyes and a short tongue.

-Russian Proverb

- Be wiser than other people, if you can, but do not tell them so.

-Lord Chesterfield

- It's better to give than to lend, and it costs about the same.

-Sir Philip Gibbs

- Never extend your hand further than you can withdraw it.

-Seumas Macmanus

- It is kindness to refuse immediately what you intend to deny.

-Martin Luther King

- Never interrupt someone doing what you said couldn't be done.

-Amelia Earhart

- The wise man in the storm prays to God, not of safety from danger, but for deliverance from fear.

-Ralph Waldo Emerson

- Not to kill is the quintessence of all wisdom. To be equal minded to all creatures and feeling oneness with all beings is Ashima. Learn this noble virtue.

-Lord Mahavira

- Silence and refusal to be drawn into conflict are formidable weapons.

-Indira Gandhi

- Don't ever take a fence down until you know the reason why it was put up.

-Gilbert Keith Chesterton

- In a verbal confrontation, lower your voice to the degree that the other person raises his or hers.

-Gore Vidal

- Praise the bridge that carried you over.

-George Colman

- The best answer to anger is silence.

-Marcus Aurelius

- When on vacation or on a family holiday, don't be too concerned about the cost. This is not a time to count pennies; it's a time to make memories.

-H. Jackson Brown Jr.

- Temptation towards too many outside interests is wrong. It is vital to eliminate the unimportant and unessential.

-Anonymous

- Rebuke with soft words and hard arguments.

–Proverb

- The ultimate wisdom is to live in the present, plan for the future and profit from the past.

-Jacob Braude

- Let no one be willing to speak ill of the absent.

-Sextus Properties

- A good man is the best friend, and, therefore, soonest to be chosen, longer to be retained and indeed, never to be parted with.

-J. Taylor

- Call on a business man at business time only and on business, transact your business and go about your business in order to give him time to finish his business.

-Duke of Wellington

· When we have not what we like, we must like what we have.

-Bussy Rabutin

· I have always been a quarter of an hour before my time, and it has made a man of me.

-Nelson Mandela

· Not to be provoked is best; but if moved, never react till the fume is spent; for every stroke our fury strikes is sure to hit ourselves at last.

-William Penn

· Praise the sea; on shore remain.

-John Florio

· If you would wish another to keep your secret, first keep it yourself.

-Seneca

· Miss not the discourse of elders.

-Ecclesiastes

· The art of being wise is the art of knowing what to overlook.

-Dale Carnegie

· Weak people take revenge. Strong people forgive. Intelligent people ignore.

-Albert Einstein

· An investment in knowledge pays the best interest.

-Benjamin Franklin

- If you cannot bite, never show your teeth.

-Anonymous

- Don't confuse mere inconveniences with real problems.

-Acharya Tulsi

- You may not control all the events that happen to you, but you can decide not to be reduced by them.

-Maya Angelou

- In the long history of humankind....those who learned to collaborate and improvise most effectively have prevailed.

-Charles Darwin

- One by one they were all becoming shades. Better pass boldly into the other world, in the full glory of some passion, than fade and wither dismally with age.

-James Joyce

- Have more than you show, speak less than you know

-William Shakespeare

- Do the difficult things while they are easy and do the great things while they are small.

-Lao Tzu

ෆ

~~~~~~

"*BEAUTY AND DUTY*

I slept and dreamed that life was beauty
I worked and found that life was duty.
Was my dream, then, a shadowy lie?

Toil on, sad hart, courageously
And thou shalt find thy dream shall be
A noon day light and a truth to thee."

-Elle Sturgis Hooper

~~~~~~

ෆ

XXV
Extras

ॐ

> "May egotism I never feel;
> Angry, may never I become;
> On seeing other worldly wealth,
> To envy may I not succumb.
> May I always feel and ponder,
> To act in true and sincere way;
> I always may do good to all,
> As far as I can every day."

ॐ

OPENING QUOTE

∞

~~~~~~

"And when you crush an apple with your teeth, say to it in your heart: your seeds shall lie in my body. And the buds of your tomorrow shall blossom in my heart. And your fragrance shall be my breath. And together we shall rejoice through all seasons."

-Kahlil Gibran

~~~~~~

∞

EXTRAS

- We can't upload luck. We can't download time. Google can't give all the answers in life. So just login to reality and realise where you stand and work hard to advance a little every day.

    -Anonymous

- Mind is not a dustbin to keep anger, hatred and jealousy. But it's a treasure box to keep love, happiness and sweet memories.

    -Anonymous

- The greatness of America lies not in being more enlightened than any other nation, but rather in her ability to repair her faults.

    -Alexis De Jocqueille

- Even if you face seemingly insurmountable challenges, always do good to others. Be selfless. Mentally remove everything and be free. This is divine life.

    -Swami Sivananda

- Woe to the man whose heart has not learned while young to hope, to love and to put its trust in life.

    -Joseph Courad

- The man who has no imagination has no wings.

    -Anonymous

- Man is a mystery. It needs to be unravelled, and if you spend your whole life unravelling it, don't say that you've wasted time.

-Fyodor Dostovesky

- Misery is the by-product of a lazy mind. Happiness is the by-product of an alert mind. Stop kicking yourself with regrets and guilt feelings. Learn from mistakes.

-Swami Sukhabodhananda

- Go often to the house of a friend; for weeds soon choke up the unused path.

-Anonymous

- He, who knows little, quickly tells it.

-Anonymous

- Examine what is said, not him who speaks it.

-Anonymous

- Two men look out through the same bars; one sees the mud and one the stars.

-Frederick Lang bridge

- The ant that breaks the line is the one that finds new sources of food for the community. Rebellion is fundamental to innovation.

-Shekhar Modi

- You can tell me about a person by what he says about others than you can by what others say about him.

-Audrey Hepburn

- You may delay, but time will not.

-Benjamin Franklin

- Great minds discuss ideas. Average minds discuss events. Small minds discuss people.

-Eleanor Roosevelt

- It is only an error in judgement to make a mistake, but it shows infirmity of character to adhere to it when discovered.

-Christian Bovee

- The past can't hurt you anymore. Not unless you let it.

-Alan Moore

- If a man lived, not according to what any priests said, but according to what seemed decent and honest inside, then it would, at the end, turn out all right.

-Terry Pritchett

- The common argument that crime is caused by poverty is a kind of slander on the poor.

-H L Mencken

- I disagree profoundly with what you say, but I shall defend to my death your right to say it.

–Voltaire

- The moral nature of a man is more scary in my eyes than his intellectual nature. I know they cannot be divorced – that without intelligence we should be brutes but goodness, lovingness and quiet self-sacrifice are worth all the talents in the world.

-George Henry Lewes

• Real generosity toward the future lies in giving all to the present.

-Albert Cames

• The important thing is not to stop questioning. Curiosity has its own reason for existing. One cannot help being in awe when he contemplates the mysteries of eternity of life, of the marvellous structure of reality.

-Albert Einstein

• Everything is valuable only in two situations. First before getting it, second after losing it. In between we do not realize the value of anything.

-Anonymous

• Nature is always giving us examples why we should never give up.

-Anonymous

• Achievers never expose themselves, but their achievements expose them.

-Anonymous

• I used to think that the worst thing in life was to end up alone. It's not. The worst thing in life is to end up with people who make you feel alone.

-Anonymous

• Presence is more than just being there.

-Malcolm S Torbes

• The deepest feeling always shows itself in silence.

-Marianne Moore

• A pessimist sees the difficulty in every opportunity; an optimist sees the opportunity in every difficulty.

-Anonymous

· Never let any idea go uncaptured.

-Anonymous

ॐ

~~~~~~

"BIRDS, STUPIDITY STREET
I saw with open eyes
Singing birds sweet
For the people to eat
Sold in the shops of
Stupidity Street."

-Ralph Hodgson

~~~~~~

ॐ

XXVI
Yours Forever

ॐ

"Kuch Likh Ke So
Kuch Padh Ke So
Jis Jagah Tu Jaaga Savere
Uss Jagah Se Kuch Badh Ke So

[<u>Translation</u>: Write something and then only you sleep
Read something and then only you sleep
Where you woke up in the morning
Advance a little from there and then only you sleep]"

-Bhawani Prasad Mishra

ॐ

OPENING QUOTE

ଐଓ

~~~~~~

"'Children's inquiries.....are often wrongly answered, and the higher the subject, the more you think yourself justified in lying to them. From these same children you expect in return truly-felt love, good acts, truthfulness and a desire to learn... you absolutely cripple a child by not allowing him to think clearly on all subjects'."

-Olga Jacoby

~~~~~~

ଐଓ

YOURS FOREVER......

A

- On your birthday, send your mother a "Thank You" card.
- Include your parents in your prayers.
- Put love notes in your child's lunch box.
- Reserve a weekly luncheon or breakfast for your spouse and children. This is more important to them than your business success.
- Never say anything uncomplimentary about your wife or children in the presence of others.
- Apologize immediately when you lose your temper, especially to children.
- Encourage your children to join a choir.
- Teach your children never to underestimate someone with a disability.
- Occasionally let your children help you, even if it slows you down.
- Don't over schedule your children's extracurricular activities.
- Require your children to do their share of household chores.
- Don't minimize your child's worries and fears.
- Say something every day that encourages your children.
- Your child will follow your example, not your advice.
- Don't take away children's dignity and their self respect.
- They are cut out for much bigger things in life. One low marks in exam would not take away their dream and talents
- To help your children turnout well, spend twice as much time with them and half as much money.

B

- Be quick to take advantage of an advantage.
- Learn to say 'no' occasionally.
- What you must do, do cheerfully.
- Remember that life's big challenges rarely give advance warning.
- Reject and condemn prejudice based on race, gender, religion or age.

- Don't forget a little kindness and don't remember a small fault.
- Trust your intuition, trust your own inner guidance, it knows best.
- In disagreements with loved ones, deal with the current situation, don't bring up the past.
- Enjoy the satisfaction that comes from doing little things well.
- When you hear a kind word spoken about a friend, tell him so.
- Forgive quickly.
- Earn your success based on service to others, not at the expense of others.
- Spend twice as much time praising as you do criticizing.
- Remember that a grateful heart is almost always a happy one.
- Never leave a loved one in anger.
- Don't get caught glancing at your watch when you're talking to someone.
- After someone apologizes to you, don't lecture him.
- When someone gives you something, never say, "you shouldn't have".
- Never resist a generous impulse.
- Fight fairly, give generously, and laugh loudly.
- Admonish your friends privately, but praise them openly.
- Take care of your body. It is the only place you live in.

"It is enough to be pleasant
When life flows along like a song:
But the man worthwhile is the one
Who will smile when everything goes dead wrong."

-Ella Wheeler Wilcox

PART - II : Prose is Architecture

ॐ

"*GHALIB YAHI KHATA TAMAAM UMRA KARTA RAHA*

DHOOL CHEHRE PE THI, AAINA SAAF KARTA RAHA

[<u>Translation</u>: THIS MISTAKE ALL MY LIFE I WENT ON DOING

DUST WAS ON THE FACE, MIRROR I KEPT ON CLEANING]"

ॐ

৪৩

<hr>

<u>OPENING QUOTE</u>

"It is not "FORGIVE AND FORGET" as if nothing wrong had ever happened, but "FORGIVE AND GO FORWARD" building on the mistakes of the past and the energy generated by reconciliation to create a new future."

-Alan Paton

<hr>

৪৩

XXVII

For Me Not To Forget Ever

"Do all the good you can, by all the means you can, in all the ways you can, in all the places you can, to all the people you can, as long as you can."

-John Wesley

FOR ME NOT TO FORGET EVER

I firmly believe in the existence of the soul and its immortality. Naturally this leads me to believe in rebirths also. My faith in all this enjoins upon me an obligation to be always noble in my thoughts, in my words and noble in my deeds. It is pretty difficult to put this into practice all the time but it is true, nevertheless, that the inner happiness springs only from remaining ever alert to this obligation.

Forgiveness is the virtue of virtues. The world has worshipped those who mastered this virtue. Every religion has preached it and religions, as we all know, have their roots in no ordinary mortals. There is therefore no reason why should we not have complete faith and confidence in the wisdom of those who found the path of mental peace and relaxed surroundings in forgetting and forgiving the faults of others. The words of Brian Tracy, "Forgiveness is a perfectly selfish act. It sets you free from the past", are worth pondering over.

Commitment to win the hearts of new acquaintances and to ever expand the circle of friends is no small earning. Friends are best assets whose sensex only rises and rises. They are always a true guide, and sweet relations and harmony are always the best shield.

No ill opinion should be formed about anyone on mere suspicions. Suspicions only haunt the mind of the suspect or without any corresponding gain. Nurturing ill feeling even towards a wrongdoer does no good to us. After all, we can not punish anyone as we wish. One should therefore leave the wrong deeds themselves to punish the doer.

Better never to lose tranquility of mind. Cool and composed posture leaves a lasting impression. A smiling face wins everyone and helps achieve the target with a better amount of certainty than any other device. It also extracts more from the opposite party than what heated exchanges can achieve.

Discussion achieves positive results and helps find right solutions. Arguments soon tempers and result in sense-blinding anger. All this ends up in accusing each other and in turning friends into foes.

Instead of allowing adversities or petty losses to hammer our thoughts all the time and halt our imagination, it is better just to forget them and concentrate on big things in our hands and on those in which lies a better future.

Even and odd go together. There is no way to choose only evens and just sidewalk the odds. We should therefore accept both as the ways of life. Even should not make us over-joyous nor do odds dampen our spirits.

Preachings and teachings of the sages and the ages remind and insist to make our lives more sublime with the passing of each day. Faith in reincarnation of the soul is the starting point towards that goal. Belief in the eternal truth that death is only a transition into some other frame of the body and, as a corollary, belief in the theory of karma keeps us right on the path to that destination.

The man should ever feel indebted to nature for the two very precious gifts it has given to him. One- there is no end to learning and we can learn something every time and from everything that comes along our way. Together with this, nature also endowed us with a zeal and a quest to always explore new horizons and go on discovering something unknown so far. We should only remember that there is no joy and pleasure greater than acquiring diversified knowledge and that we should never allow the zeal and quest, which opens new vistas before us, to lie dormant.

The other one is that there is nothing on this earth which is useless or a sheer waste. Every object we see here, whatever be its form or frame, exists with an object and with a purpose. Nature gave us insight and imagination to find that purpose and to think of the use we can make even of what looks worth not caring for. Here again we need to be alert not to allow our insight and inquisitiveness to ever go into slumber.

I was looking for the words to conclude these lines which are addressed to me more than to anyone else, but was stuck for a while. Suddenly a small couplet from Acharya Mahapragya's great epic 'Rishbhayan' flashed in my mind. It instantly convinced me that I would not find a better conclusion than the soul-searching message which the couplet carries and conveys-

"*Satya itna hi nahi*
jitna ki main hoon Maanta
Vyom utna hi nahi
jitna ki mai hoon jaanta
Yeh aseem, ise na apne
sadan tak seemit karo,
par sadan mein bhi gagan hai,
satya ko sweekrit karo.

[<u>Translation</u>: Truth isn't only that much which I believe. The space and sky isn't only that much which I know. Reality is infinite, let us not limit it within our confines. Even what seem like confines also have expansive skies, that must be accepted as the truth.]"

XXVIII
Honour The Time

癰

~~~~~~

<u>OPENING QUOTE</u>

"I expect to pass through this world but once. Any good thing, therefore, that I can do, or any kindness that I can show to any fellow creature, let me do it now..... for I shall not pass this way again."

-S. Grellet

~~~~~~

癰

HONOUR THE TIME

The bounties of nature are immense. They are immeasurable. The life, the life-like earth, the life-sky and the wonderful contrasts occupying all these – contrasts of the corpulent and the sublime, of the moving and the static, of the mystic and the manifest! All so fascinating and so beautifully laid in perfect harmony with no chaos, confusion or conflict in between.

There is, however, one thing nature has been miser in blessing the man with and that is time. The hours in a day are limited, the days in a year are limited and years in our life are limited. Viewed this way, time is the scarcest thing at man's disposal and therefore the most precious. Yet he spends it most prodigally and most wastefully. What is still more unfortunate is that most of us do not even realize how unwisely and unknowingly we allow it to slip out of our hands unutilized.

Kay Lyons has said "yesterday is a cancelled cheque, tomorrow is a promissory note and today is the only cash you have". The only day of any importance in one's life is today. Tomorrow is a tricky illusion. The promises of tomorrow are seldom whole hearted. Let us therefore sit today. Today itself makes us available to learn from the experiences and expressions of the wise, who thought of time as a priceless possession and who saw it passing fast and based on this realization who learned to command it.

Time is something whole. Management of time is therefore management of the whole. Management of time enables one to develop his faculties and make full use of his potential. Management of time is, in fact, management of life and is therefore an art to be perfected. It simply means installing a regulator in life to strike a balance in all its manifestations – emotional, behavioural and functional.

"I am horribly busy "or "I did not get time" – Such claims are often an unconscious admission of inability and lack of competence. It is basic therefore to first realize where we lack and where we fritter away the time. We spend eight hours on our prime job and require eight hours of sleep and another four hours for eating, dressing, moving to and from, etc. We still have four hours or at least three hours in hand left daily. To this may be added other free hours of Sundays and other holidays. Just a little calculation and we will know that hours of spare time in a week is easily twenty hours which we can utilize in other creative pursuits.

A valid argument obstructs our way here. One needs rest and relaxation, recreational pastimes, reading newspapers and magazines. Accommodating social calls also demand their dues. Remaining indifferent to the obligations of hospitality is also not easy. When to do all this if there is no spare time? This is right. But we have only to pause and think whether we are rightly using our time in these pursuits. Relaxation should not be confused with idleness. It means relieving tension. We can make the work itself a source of relieving tension, if we develop a fondness for the job in hand and do it with full interest.

Light material magazines and newspapers are produced with rapidity and should also be read with rapidity. Newspapers can be glanced through in work interludes or while waiting for something or in other blank periods. At social functions, we should try to meet with experienced and learned persons. Discoursing and exchanging views with such persons is quite a gainful employment of time. Hospitality also does not mean observing long formalities and allowing the visitor to steal our time as he wishes, just as it is not wise to always stand during ceremonies.

Even six, seven or eight spare hours a week is an enormous time. But it is melted away commonly in excessive sleep, engaging in petty works which could well be delegated to others, waiting for the tea to arrive offered unnecessarily to a visitor dropping in just for nothing, gossiping on no-sense subjects, flirting with a magazine or to watching a day long cricket match glued to TV or sometimes simply idling. At the workplace too, time is wasted in rewriting letters first dictated without full facts, in waiting for a file which should have been on the table before, in the staff interrupting too often for seeking clarifications on issues which should have been elaborately explained at the start or in stretching ten minutes coffee break to half an hour gossip or in just searching out files, papers, equipment and appliances not kept carefully.

The most painful waste of time is also on a different count and that is indecisiveness. Moving the thoughts just forth and back without settling down either 'Yes' or on 'No' is not playing fair game with time. The art of learning to quickly choose between the alternatives is the art of all arts. To decide fast about what to do, when to do and to get into the inappropriate frame of mind for productive work ensures proper use of time.

The examples cited above are just illustrative. A close observation of one's own habits and his own surroundings will reveal the spots responsible for waste of time affecting him.

Let us now concentrate on factors fundamental in time planning. The basic points may be counted as under:

1. Punctuality is the starting point. It means moving in harmony with the steps of time. Time does not remain in good company of those who cannot keep appointments or too often fail to maintain schedules.

2. Budgeting the daily time and allocating it to the day's work with an intention to stick to it is the second step. This done, it should be given the force of law which should not be disobeyed.

3. Planning an over-crowded day causes tension and results in early fatigue. There should be some breathing space in switching over from one job to another. This also allows us to accommodate unexpected calls and emergencies.

4. Regular daily work instills a sense of competence and confidence. This eventually results in more output and saves time.

5. 'One thing at a time' is the golden rule. Diversion to other matters, leaving the work in hand half-done, is the wrong way of handling things.

6. Priorities should be determined. To ensure better concentration on serious matters, it is advisable to finish easy and low-time demanding things at the start.

7. Keeping a broad general picture of the work in view and long range objectives in memory enables the unconscious mind to detect flaws and eliminate errors. It ensures timely performance too.

8. Temptations towards too many outside interests are wrong. It is vital to eliminate the unessential and unimportant.

9. Entangling in too many details, lengthy enquiries into trifles and involvement in wrong type of work or at wrong stage takes heavy toll of time with little gains in return.

10. Terminating overlong conversations, lengthy arguments and unnecessary interruptions without this being felt by the person involved is a skill. Not allowing others to steal our time is important.

11. Knowing one's own limitations in terms of resources, time and energy helps in not going stray or awry. The work should be planned within these limitations. It is no use making grandiose plans which can never be put into effect.

12. Ensuring right infrastructure and proper arrangements that permit uninterrupted concentrations during the period of actual work immensely save time, labour and cost.

13. Reading self-development course books and quotes of the great thinkers and doers enhances knowledge and experience which can act as a true guide in all spheres throughout life. Acquiring diversified knowledge in spare moments and learning from the wisdom of others yield a rich harvest.

14. The best way of spending spare time is to devote it to certain works of art or beauty or usefulness so that one satisfies not only one's creative urge but also produces something of value to the society. Four-five hours a week taken from frivolous pursuits and profitably employed enables any man of ordinary prudence to master a complete art.

Listen to the whisper of the moment-
'Time rewards them who honour every minute of the hour, every hour of the day and every day of the year." **LISTEN!**

XXIX
I Have Not Failed

OPENING QUOTE

"WHEN YOU LOSE, DON'T LOSE THE LESSON."

-The Dalai Lama

I HAVE NOT FAILED

Positive and negative are forces opposite to each other. But under some mysterious arrangement of nature, they acted in unison in creating this universe and are doing so in maintaining a fine balance between the entire existence. The interconnection and the interdependence of the opposites dominate everywhere and contrasts complete the circle. That is why action prompts reaction, cause results in effect and matter exists with antimatter.

Each one of us also reflects this inherent duality of the cosmos. For every strength that we possess, we also have some inevitable weakness. The basic aim of progress is to overcome our weakness and garner our strength. So if we have made mistakes, instead of concentrating on the mistakes themselves, we should tackle the misjudgement and learn from the errors which caused them. Thomas Alva Edison said "I have not failed, I have just found 10,000 ways that won't work". This expresses Edison's focus on keeping his imagination flying and his ideas moving. That is the human spirit we should also always keep high.

We should never mind if something goes wrong at one time or the other. It happens with everyone including the most experienced ones. What we have to understand is that realisation of past mistakes and failures is part of our own growing up; it is part of our updated wisdom. No one can evolve without making mistakes. All we have to do is to try to find better alternatives and imagine how improvement is possible even in traditional and well accepted ways of life and work.

Feelings of guilt are totally negative and retarding. Always regretting the past errors and lapses only spoils the value of the present. It is really sad that distortion of religions, stale social customs, blind rituals and dogma conspire to breed guilt in us, so that they can rule us. We should be cautious and alert about such evils and cant phraseology which intends to instill blind faith and foster fanaticism. Prudency demands that we test things on the scale of logic and interpret them applying our own mind.

Lies, distorting or exaggerating the facts are all aspects of falsehood which lower our image in the estimation of others and cost us our reliability. Lies have a short life. Soon the truth reveals itself putting us in an uneasy and awkward situation. It is therefore of primary importance to practice integrity of speech. We should always mean what we say and do what we promise.

Here it will be worthwhile to talk a little bit about the two most common causes which make us commit mistakes. One is haste. Hurriedly trying to complete varieties of work in a short time renders our senses off balance and shrinks our thinking power. Over-haste therefore never fastens the work. On the contrary, it adversely affects our judgement and slows down the pace in the end result. The errors of Judgement invite mistakes, which make us repent later. The only right way is to start well in advance and finish the work while the smile is on the lips and before tension takes over.

The other one is anger. Anger starts with folly and straightaway takes us to the borders of insanity for the time we are in grip of it. Unable to distinguish between right and wrong, whatever we say or do in anger is always something for which we have to regret and repent sooner or later. It is wise therefore not to lose temper for everything that does not go as we wish.

'To err is human' is an old dictum. It is true to its root. But with a little amount of patience and with a ready willingness to understand the views of others, we can guard ourselves against any misdeal or misadventure or misjudgement. And then it would be easy to win in the tests of life. It is also worthwhile here to have a look on the words of Roy H Williams-

> *"A smart man makes a mistake, learns from it and never makes that mistake again.*
> *But a wise man finds a smart man and learns from him how to avoid the mistake altogether."*

XXX

Outward To Inward To Onward

&

OPENING QUOTE

"The two most important days in your life are the days you are born and the day you find out why."

-Mark Twain

&

OUTWARD TO INWARD TO ONWARD

It happens at times that even some basic recipes vital for a successful, happy and relaxed life unknowingly sunk in our unconscious mind and are lost sight of while dealing with the present day perplexities and confusions. What I write here is neither new nor unknown to anyone, yet I thought it worthwhile to write these lines just to reassure that they always remain firmly rooted in our conscious mind.

1.

The art of observation is the art of all arts. It is the ignition switch that sets the imagination off the launching pad. Imagination, in its turn, arouses inquisitiveness and then, by searching answers for "WHY and HOW" and by asking questions about the ordinary things, we slip into extraordinary thoughts and get extraordinary ideas and discover extraordinary things. Ideas keep us moving on the path and process of evolution.

We should, however, not be in a hurry to push the bare bone of an idea. It is vital to review and re-evaluate the idea in leisure time with a free mind to make it conform to the standards of art or science.

2.

Listening is a great virtue. It is a quality of life no less valuable and no less rewarding than the art of observation. It is an act of courtesy. It also enriches one with the views, ideas and wisdom of others. But there is an art to listening. Unfortunately most of us listen through a screen of resistance. We are screened with prejudices, - religious or psychological or of our daily worries, desires and fears. Therefore, we listen to our own sound, to our own noise, not to what is being said. For objective listening we must hear the other person without imposing our preconceived notions or opinions. Having listened, we can summarise, digest and evaluate what is of importance or what is of use to us.

3.

Determination is the basic requirement for success in any field. We should proceed with a firm resolution, full confidence and go to work with a cheerful frame of mind. Things seem difficult only at the start and only when attended to half-heartedly. If we try to understand the job in hand inside out and involve ourselves earnestly in anything that comes along the way, it readily reveals all its secrets. Everything then looks not only easy but inviting and interesting as well. Having good general knowledge also makes difficult targets achievable.

4.

Rigved says "Shabd Brahma Hai". Science echoes the meaning of this when it tells us that sound is eternal and every word uttered remains in the ether and gets a matching vibration from the universe. The vibration of sound creates material reality. We should understand this phenomena and train ourselves to think precisely and speak effectively. The words of Evangel- 'Wisdom is knowing when to speak your mind and when to mind your speech' - are worth pondering over.

5.

As thoughts determine actions, there is a powerful connection between words we use and results we get. Our words should therefore be compassionate and encouraging and of hope and joy. Flexible and adaptable attitude wins every heart. It also helps gain social support. Being courteous and polite and talking in a soft voice make two people get along better.

6.

We should avoid words which hurt and humiliate, even if provoked. When angry, it is better to stop speaking or change the subject of discussion. A serious talk may be lightened up by an effective use of humour, but in making humorous cracks, we should avoid offending any member of the audience. While in an assembly, we should speak only when we are confident that our words will be better than our silence. Our words should complement our thoughts and actions and our conversation should be a two way dialogue with both sides communicating.

7.

A good decision has to be prompt, firm and correct and should pass the logical test of being thoughtful and rational. There should also be consistency in decisions. Having once taken, we should be slow in changing it. Decision should be followed by efforts to achieve the objective it was meant to achieve. Yet it should not be imposed on anyone not readily agreeing with it.

8.

Remaining undue panicky about health is bad but to be health conscious is good. Diseases which come of their own, despite following general health rules, are normally easy to cure.But the ailments which set in due to negligence, carelessness, overwork, tension or wrong eating habits often stay long.

9.

Writing should not be clumsy. Unclear notings on paper are often confusing even to the writer himself and consume a lot of time in decoding. After use, keep all things like mobile phones, spectacles, wrist watch, punching, staple and scissors etc. and office files at some definite spot earmarked for them. Methodical work and neat and tidy habits pay far more than what they cost in terms of time or energy.

10.

Children in their age cannot distinguish between right and wrong. They only learn from us and pick our habits. It is vital therefore that we present before them an ideal way of living. Our thoughts, our speech, our conduct and our behaviour should all come to them as a good teacher, a good guide and a good friend. AND here from starts the journey onwards.

XXXI

The Chess Of Whims & Pleasures

&

<u>OPENING QUOTE</u>

"Time goes, you say? Ah, nol Alas, time stays, we go."

-Austin Dobson

&

THE CHESS OF WHIMS & PLEASURES

We were classmates in our school days, in the early fifties. After completing the school final, I proceeded East and he went to the North to pursue college studies. Years rolled by. We did not see each other. The other day I most unexpectedly met him at an airport while I was stuck there waiting for my delayed flight. The meeting was short lived but immensely refreshing.

I boarded my plane and settled down on my seat. Seemingly everything was settled in my mind too. But some abstract thoughts suddenly stormed it-as suddenly as that meeting itself came. A question haunted me -at whose whims we abruptly parted with each other some sixty years ago and at whose pleasure we met again in a most surprising manner after the lapse of such a long period? A whisper sounded close to my ears - "It is time, my friend, it is time". I was convinced perhaps. So my thoughts took liberty to travel on the wheels of time for a little while more.

The giant dinosaurs once ruled the earth with complete authority. They perished suddenly. The great Roman Empire lost its pomp and glory even before the Romans could know what wrong besieged them. Jupiter swallowed the comet Shoemaker-Levy leaving no trace of it. All this not so quite good at whose whims? Now look here. It is a different sight on this side. A killer dacoit Valmiki tums into a great poet and a pious sage. An abandoned and stray drop of rain finds shelter in an oyster and grows into a shining pearl. The moon is barren-barren of violence, barren of untruthfulness; barren of all the vices the man has made this earth hang its head in shame in the fraternity of its fellow planets. All this so very lovely at whose pleasure? I hear the same whisper-"It is time." I am convinced this time too. Yes, it is time alone which makes and unmakes. Yes, it is time alone which is noble and harsh, kind and cruel, benign and malignant at once.

Time is something strange indeed. It sees Räm killing Ravan. It sees with equal ease Godse killing Gandhi. A sordid contrast! How curious? How stupid? But only to me and you. Time remains unruffled, undisturbed, unconceded on both the occasions. Whether the man passing into it is a Ravan or a Gandhi, it is no difference to it.

Time-invisible yet almighty. Invisible yet the seed of all that occupies this universe-whether corpulent or subline, moving or static, manifest or mystic. What is this time? How it passes with the earth rotating around the sun? Why can't we catch it on back gear? Why it destroys its own creations? Why a futile mental exercise on the mysteries of time brings a smile on our lips in contrast to the frustration and disappointment which failure to solve other problems causes in our mind? Time really provides stuff for most interesting study and the more one thinks over it, the deeper its secrets seem to go. And that is one reason why I feel the person unfolding its mystery will be doing more harm than good by closing a most interesting and absorbing chapter the man has been lured to ever since his birth. For, once the man has known the secrets of time and its offshoot the life itself, inside out and upside down, what else he will live for or for that matter, what he will be afraid of to die then?

I am not venturing to talk on a subject too big for the size of me. But, in the lines to follow, I do intend to give a glimpse of the wonder that was India in the time that is past and gone. I am also not venturing to catch time on back gear. Yet I will take you some eight hundred years down the ladder of time when this land used to be inhabited by people who cared for their country and put some earnest efforts to make it immortal.

Sometime back, I went on an excursion tour of South India and visited, inter- alia, Mysore, Belur and Halebidu. The first one, as you know, is a famous city while the latter two obscure villages situated about 100 kilometers away from Mysore. Among the places seen at Mysore. I shall make particular mention of the palace of Maharaja of Mysore. The Indian Maharajas have been famous the world over for their lavish spending and luxurious living a few in history have been able to afford. The palace is a fine specimen of that princely poop and grandeur. It is a massive construction built magnificently with costliest materials. A gold, silver and sandalwood extravaganza with precious articles it houses in, including two solid gold thrones weighing about three hundred kilos, it can quite be an object of envy. But that is what money can conveniently buy and riches can always have. In contrast, I shall now take you to an art treasure which only complete dedication, total devotion and untiring zeal can produce. And that is what the said two villages Belur and Halebidu-store in the shape of two temples.

Both the temples were built about eight hundred years ago by a queen, herself a great dancer, named Shantala of Hoyshala Dynasty. The Halebidu temple was completed in one hundred ten years by three generations of sculptors and the temple at Belur in one hundred ninety years by five generations of them. But the architectural beauty which now stands there is worth many times more the time taken. Stone has been cut and carved like wood, if not paper and one really wonders how they could make it possible with just ordinary chisels. The engineering skill displayed there can really eclipse the best architectural talents of the day. Each temple consists of about ten thousand sculptures big and small and is a matchless monument of intrinsic art which keeps one spell-bound and leaves dazed. The imagination is wonderful, execution perfect; the theme choice is marvelous, presentation lively, the craftsmanship is superb and above all their patience infinite

Art and craft, beauty and bounty, care and commitment, dedication and devotion and persistence and patience embodied and alive in Belur and Halebidu temples of the 12th century at whose pleasure? Capitalism and communism, chaos and confusion, contempt and corruption, crimes and cruelties and conspiracies and the crowded courts of the 21st century at whose whims? The whisper rings into my ears a different tune now-"It is not time, my friend, not the time. Man must look at himself. Man owes to look at himself. The next dawn can be the dawn of heaven here if only the man so tries. If only the man so wishes. This earth is beautiful but sad looking at the man whimsically letting the hell rule on this lovely planet

The whisper continues-"Can't the man take command of these whims and pleasures? Can't the man make this earth too barren of violence and untruthfulness? Can't the man see his destiny in one world, one faith and one ism?"

The whisper is more assertive and imposing this time. It wins me over. It makes me aver and echo its sentiments-This earth is beautiful but sad. Must not the man realize it? Must not the man listen to this message of Frank Borman* which is still floating in the air-"The view of the earth from the moon fascinated me-a small disc, 240,000 miles away. Raging nationalistic interests, famines, wars, pestilence don't show from that distance......"? Must not the man underline the core meaning of this communiqué sent by Borman from the moon?

We owe it to ourselves not to let the wisdom of queen Shantala, Austin Dobson, Benjamin Franklin and Frank Borman vanish in wilderness.

PART - III : Poetry Is Interior Decoration

The ensuing pages are a bouquet of colourful poems which sound like musical thoughts and unveil truth dwelling in beauty.

৪৩

"*Poets are the mirrors of the gigantic shadows which futurity casts upon the present; the words which express what they understand not; the trumpets which sing to battle, and feel not what they inspire; the influence which is moved not but moves.... Poets are the unacknowledged legislators of the world.*"

-Percy Bysshe Shelley

৪৩

XXXII
Human Family

"I note the obvious differences
In the human family.

Some of us are serious,
Some thrive on comedy.

Some declare their lives are lived
As true profundity,
And others claim they really live
The real reality

The variety of our skin tones
Can confuse, bemuse, delight,
Brown and pink and beige and purple,
Tan and blue and white.

I've sailed upon the seven seas
And stopped in every land,
I've seen the wonders of the world
Not yet one common man.

I know ten thousand women
Called jane and mary jane,
But I've not seen any two

Who really were the same.

Mirror twins are different
Although their features jibe,
And lovers think quite different thoughts
While lying side by side.

We love and lose in china,
We weep on england's moors
And laugh and moan in guinea
And thrive on Spanish shores.

We seek success in finland,
Are born and die in maine.
In minor ways we differ,
In major we're the same.

I note the obvious differences
Between each sort and type,
But we are more alike, my friends,
Than we are unalike.

We are more alike, my friends,
Than we are unlike."

-Maya Angelou

ೞ

XXXIII
In Spite Of War

"In spite of war, in spite of death,
In spite of all man's sufferings,
Something within me laughs and sings
And I must praise with all my breath.
In spite of war, in spite of hate
Lilacs are blooming at my gate,
Tulips are tripping down the path
In spite of war, in spite of wrath.
"Courage!" the morning-glory saith
"Rejoice!" the daisy murmureth,
And just to live is so divine
When pansies lift their eyes to mine.

The clouds are romping with the sea
And flashing waves call back to me
That naught is real but what is fair,
That everywhere and everywhere
A glory liveth through despair.
Though guns may roar and cannon boom;
Roses are born and gardens bloom.
My spirit still may light its flame
At that same torch whence poppies came.
Where morning's altar whitely burns
Lilies may lift their silver urns

In spite of war, in spite of shame.

And in my ear a whispering breath
"Wake from the nightmare! Look and see
That life is naught but ecstasy
In spite of war, in spite of death!"

-Angela Morgan

XXXIV

God's Flight

"On the ground sits a bird
That's too afraid to fly.
Beautiful wings could make it soar,
But the pain of past failure is its lonesome cry.

God has said unto this bird,
"Trust and have faith in me,
For I will carry you in your flight,
The miracle of life is waiting for you to see."

The bird said to God, "But I can't fly.
I am weak, I will fall and feel pain.
It's happened before when I tried to fly,
I'm afraid of being hurt again."

His voice soft and reassuring, God said to the bird,
"I created you, and I will protect you.
Your lonesome cry I have heard,
Have faith in me, that's all you need to do.

So, stand up, bird, and spread your wings,
The wings I lovingly created to let you fly.
If you fall I'll pick you up,
And lift you back into the sky."

With trembling legs and unsure wings,
The bird finally looked to the sky.
It took a deep breath, and took the chance,
The bird began to fly.

"Thank you, God, for believing in me,
Thank you for giving me wings.
Thank you for your protecting hands,
Your glory I will now sing."

God smiled unto the bird
In its majestic flight,
"little bird, I'll always be with you,
And will protect you with all my might.

You may stumble, you may fall,
That doesn't mean that I don't care.
I will watch over you, in case you need help,
And then I'll be right there."

The little bird, once so scared,
Learned to soar to new heights.
The occasional fall no longer scared the bird
Choosing to have faith in God's flight."

-Heather Flood

XXXV
A Spiritual Journey

"*Across from the mountains*
A little house sits in the trees,
I'm lost in tranquillity
As my soul tries to breathe.

White clouds moving slowly,
The breeze a calm still,
I'm caught in the moment
As my heart starts to heal.

A piece of me
In the startling blue sky,
As I spread my wings,
My soul starts to fly.

I fly to unknown places
Where pain and hurt once dwelled.
As the memories flow past me,
My eyes start to swell.

Tear drops drip slowly
Down my cheeks.
The wind wipes them dry
And gives me some peace.

Soaring so free
Over water and land,
My spirit guide gently,
Takes me by my hand.

He shows me what was
And what's meant to be,
And why my life
Is so important it seems.

A longer soar
Like the eagle high
I bow my head
And I start to cry

Back on the land
Across from the trees,
I began to realize
What healing means.

It means not to forget
Let the past flow,
Of all the horrors,
One soul had to go.

To take the strengths
And apply them to life,
Is a valuable lesson,
I've learnt this flight.

Alone in the sunset
I watch it go down,
When I finally realize
What peace I have found."

-Ana Lei Somerville

XXXVI
Wander-Thirst

"Beyond the East the sunrise, beyond the west the sea,
And east and west the wander-thirst that will not let me be.
It works in me like madness, dear, to bid me say good-bye;
For the seas call, and the stars call, and oh; the call of the sky.

.

I know not where the white road runs, nor what the blue hills are,
But a man can have the sun for a friend, and for his guide a star,
And there's no end of voyaging when once the voice is heard'
For the rivers call, and the roads call, and oh; the call of the bird;

.

Yonder the long horizon lies, and there be night and day,
The old ships draw to home again, the young ships sail away,
And come I may, but go I must, and if men ask you why,
You may put the blame on the stars and the sun
And the white road and the sky."

-Gerard Gould

XXXVII
To Remember Me

*"Give my sight to the
man who has never
seen a sunrise, a
baby's face or love in
the eyes of a woman.*

*Give my heart to a
person whose own
heart has caused
nothing but endless
days of pain.*

*Give my blood to the
teenager who was pulled from the
wreckage of his car
ss that he might live
to see his grandchildren play.*

*Take my bones, every
muscle, every fibre
and nerve in my body
and find a way to
make a crippled child walk.*

Burn what is left of me
and scatter the ashes
to the winds
to help
the flowers grow.

If you must bury
something, let it be
my faults, my weaknesses
and all prejudices against
my fellow men.

If, by chance, you
wish to remember me,
do it with a kind
deed or word to someone who needs you.

If you do all I have asked,
I will leave forever. (Abridged)"

-Robert N. Test

XXXVIII

Mother

"They say there is never a time, nor a sun
To tell when a mother's day is done.

From cleaning up and making the beds
To plaiting and combing those curly heads.

Something for breakfast, dinner and lunch
A tasty snack with tea, to munch.

Rushing out to the department store
Returning with rations, provisions and more.

Tidying the house, washing the dishes
Servant on holiday, against your wishes.

Toning, darning or embroidery work
Little things, which others might shirk.

There is no time, there is no sun
To tell when a mother's day is done."

-Anonymous

૭૭

~~~~~~

Nasti matrisama chhaya, Nasti matrsama gati
Nasti matrisamam tran, Nasti matrisama priya

.

[*Translation*: There is no shelter like mother, there is no inspiration like mother, there is no saviour like mother, there is none dearer than mother.]

~~~~~~

૭૭

XXXIX
Only A Dad

"*Only a Dad with a tired face,*
coming home from the daily race,
bringing little of gold or fame
to show how well he has played the game.
but glad in his heart that his own rejoice
to see him come and to hear his voice.

Only a Dad but he gives his all,
to smooth the way for his children small.
doing with courage, steers and grim
the deeds that his father did for him.
this is the line that for him I pen,
only A Dad, but the best of Men."

-Edgar Guest

ೞ

ॐ

~~~~~~

Observe the commandment of your father and do not forsake the teaching of your mother, bind them continually on your heart... when you walk about, they will guide you; when you sleep, they will watch over you.... for the commandment is a lamp and the teaching is light.

-Proverbs, 6-20-23

~~~~~~

ॐ

The Book's Vision In A Picture

Let Noble Thoughts Come To Us From All Directions -rig veda

AUTHOR BIO

Jatanlal Rampuria, Advocate

<u>ADDRESS</u>
15, Noormahal Lohia Lane
2nd Floor, Kolkata - 700007

.

<u>MOBILE</u>
+91-84908-20429

.

<u>PREVIOUS PUBLICATIONS</u>
>Anukriti (Hindi)
>Shrey Ka Srijan (Hindi)
>Ujale Ka Apaharan (Hindi)
>Yours Forever
>Several articles published in various
newspapers and magazines